The Creator's Temporary

On Assignment

We have a mission in this life, it is not impossible, and you will not self-destruct.

To Gen Davis;
my daughter of the Heart
may God forever Bless you.
Amelia "Micki" Carpenter
1-24-21

Amelia "Micki" Carpenter

ISBN 978-1-0980-6627-7 (paperback)
ISBN 978-1-0980-6628-4 (digital)

Christian Faith Publishing, Inc.
832 Park Avenue
Meadville, PA 16335
www.christianfaithpublishing.com

Printed in the United States of America

In service for the King of kings
(On temporary assignment to bring hope to the hopeless and
the brokenhearted. To encourage, lift spirits, and to raise faith
in a God who is the commander of the angel armies.)
All of these stories are true; only some of the names
have been changed to protect the persons involved.

Contents

Preface

Working for the King in my journey through life, I became one of the Creator's temporary on assignment. The mission is not impossible, and the adventure will not self-destruct. In these encounters, I will share times of adventure, pain, restoration, even modern-day miracles. Everyone has a purpose in life, if you are willing to accept the assignment.

"But you are the ones chosen by God, chosen for the high calling of priestly work, chosen to be a holy people, God's instrument to do His work and speak out for Him, to tell others of the night and day difference He made for you—from nothing to something, from rejected to accepted" (1 Peter 2:9 MSG; The Message provided by Eugene H. Peterson).

1. *Nobody Ever Told Me.* Kristen was kidnapped and horrified. Suddenly remembering God could hear her prayers anywhere, anytime, she prayed for the very first time and lived to tell the story.

2. *The Wrong Place at the Right Time.* In a rainstorm, the car approaching a curve veered off the road and flew up a telephone pole guide wire. A man fell through the rear window of the car before the car came crashing down. The

fast-growing crowd knew the man was dying, but God had other plans.

3. *Runaways—Far from Home.* When Reggie and Susan—teenagers—decided to run away and get married, they ended up in Florida. They were soon broke, hungry, discouraged, and still single. When they were almost arrested, God changed their lives.

4. *Where, Oh, Where Can She Be.* Daisy, a middle-aged woman, had not seen her runaway daughter, Nancy, in fifteen years. Nancy, at fifteen years old, was last seen speeding away in a car with a stranger. That was the last of it. No one had a clue where Nancy was except God.

5. *But God.* Tess and JJ had lost everything—their jobs, their home, their children—all because of drugs and alcohol. Living on the streets trying to survive in the freezing chill of winter, they had to have help or die. They reached out their hands in hope, and a merciful and loving God reached down to them.

6. *Where Is God.* Donnie and Hannah had a beautiful and happy life, until tragedy struck, and their world crumbled around them. The heartaches, the questions, the gossips, the doubts, and the innocence and guilt swept into their lives like a flood. Some people helped, and others hated. It seemed like even God couldn't be found, but He was there.

7. *Her Name Was Elizabeth.* Elizabeth had a mother who did not love her, a stepfather who abused her sexually, and a quack doctor who declared her mentally challenged and dangerous at seven years old. She was kept locked in her room. A hopeless and desperate individual, she grew up

with all of these things hidden in her mind, never telling anyone. When she was twenty-four years old, her past, present, and future changed forever because someone listened to her story.

8. *Brave and Bold.* Larry was handsome, wealthy, had his own business, and was divorced. He was also an alcoholic and my new boss. The adventures, the women, the long stories he would tell me sitting in front of my desk all played a tremendous part in this story. When he told me that he was going up (meaning heaven) when he dies, it was all I could take. A holy boldness filled my being, and I stood up, put my hands on my desk, looked him in the eyes, and told him he was headed to hell. He was aghast, and I thought I would definitely lose my job. God knows when it is time to be a bold witness.

9. *The Happiness Miracle.* Seven-year-old Roy was the outcast of his family. He was unloved, unwanted, and lonely. When a stranger invited him to church, his life changed forever. He loved the kind people, the music, and the message. Soon he came to know a loving Savior, who miraculously gave him the desires of his heart.

10. *Monster or Miracle.* Marci loved Halloween; not just the night celebration but all year long. She lived in a spooky house with all kinds of evil decorations surrounding it, not like ghosts and witches but like demons and devils. I had no desire to make her acquaintance, but when my grandson, Chris, decided to make it on his own, he ended up moving in with Marci. I wanted to beg God to let me off of this assignment, but when it came to Chris, I had

no choice. I entered into a darkness with demonic spirits, deliverance, and eventually, death. I never regretted it, and this assignment was one of the greatest in my adventures. It could have been called "snatching their souls from hell."

11. *Best Friends Forever.* Flo was a typical country mother with two small children. She was unfriendly, although she lived in our neighborhood. I tried to make friends and, somehow, just couldn't give up even when she chose to ignore me. God works in mysterious ways, for sure, when He had our children bring us together for a lifelong friendship.

12. *Adventures at the Volcano.* Not many people actually get to look inside the mouth of an active volcano. My sister, Becky, and I along with a few girlfriends took the opportunity to do so. We were on the mountaintop until we found we couldn't make it down the mountain. God still rumbles the Earth.

13. *Assignments and Adventures on My Own Personal Life.*

Acknowledgments

I would like to dedicate this book, first of all, to my mother, Sadie Harstin Barker, who always inspired me, as she would push me into situations to make me stronger; she encouraged me to write and build my faith in knowing that, with God, nothing is impossible. She expressed her love to me in so many ways; she was a wonderful mother and always my best friend. My dedication is also to my dad, Johnnie A. Barker, who was a World War II decorated hero and a hero in the army of the Lord and a hero to his family—a leader of courage always.

Next, I would like to thank my husband, Charles E. Carpenter, who was patient with me while I was writing. Sometimes, I would meet him in the hallway as he was getting up for the day, and I was finally heading to the bed to sleep. He is a wonderful father to my children and husband to me. He is "Pawpaw Charlie" to our grandchildren and great-grandchildren. His character as "Professor Diddledaddle" in our many children's crusades was an inspiration to the young and old alike. He played a leading role in one of my Christmas productions as Jeremiah in *Something's Going on in the Stable* and also major roles in many others.

Thirdly, I dedicate this book to my two precious sons, Hubert C. Jenkins, Jr. called Butch, referred to in my book as "Bruce," and Richard Scott Jenkins, referred to as "Ricky" in my book. Both sons played a major part in my life and are included with me in several of these stories. Also, to my grandson, Hubert C. Jenkins III, called Cliff, who has lived with me many years of his life and been a great inspiration to me. He is referred to as "Chris" in an event of this book.

Lastly, I dedicate this book to my sisters. To Becky Erickson, who played a major role in one of my Christmas drama production. Becky now plays my cohost in the productions of *Blanche and Maggie*, a Christian comedy team of two now being performed in various churches and groups in North Carolina and South Carolina. Becky is my inspiration in getting all of this together; she encouraged me, helped me, proofread *The Creator's Temporary*, and pushed me to finish and get it published. Also, to my sisters, Kathy Taylor and Crystal Rose, who have played many leading roles in my Christmas drama productions and many events in my life.

Most of all, I dedicate this book with thanks and praise to my Father God and my loving Savior, Jesus Christ, my guide, my inspiration, my courage, and my strength, who made these events and this book possible. Without Him, I could do nothing. When the Almighty says, "Who's available?" I reply, "Send me." The unimaginable happens according to His will, and a purpose is fulfilled.

I could not end this dedication without giving appreciation to the many characters who have touched my life in the exciting stories which occurred in the events of *The Creator's Temporary*. As you read them, you will fully understand why some names have been changed, but I remember every one of them personally as I remember the events that changed their lives and mine. God used just an ordinary girl who loves Him and the people He sent me to. Some are still living and remembering these events with me; some have passed on to their eternal homes to spend forever with God, our Creator, and Jesus, the King of kings.

1

"Nobody Ever Told Me"

It was the first day on my job in a new city. I was excited and a little nervous as Hugh took me around the office to introduce me to my associates. Everyone seemed very nice and greeted me with welcoming smiles—that is, until I met Kristen.

"Now, this is Kristen, and you will be working very close with her in the word processing department." Hugh led me through the portal that sectioned off our working area.

"Kristen, here's your new partner." Hugh beamed. "This is Amelia, but she prefers to be called 'Micki' by her friends."

I held out my hand to greet her.

"I really don't care what you prefer to be called." She snarled. "I just hope you are not a religious fanatic like the last woman who worked here."

She extended a weak handshake to greet me. I did my best to put forth a smile and took a few seconds to look over my new associate. She was in her early thirties, short blond hair, with huge blue eyes, and a skinny, frail frame. Before I could respond with an answer, Hugh spoke to us.

"I will leave it to you, girls." He paused. "Micki, I am sure Kristen will be able to answer any questions you may have." He cheerfully walked away.

"Well, girl, tell me about yourself, and I will tell you about the work we have to do in this department. Everything is a rush, and everybody wanted it yesterday, know what I mean?"

I managed a slight grin.

"Yes, I am familiar with that situation." I chuckled.

"Well, now, about me, we just moved to Orlando about a month ago from North Carolina. I'm married, have two wonderful little boys, ages six and eight, and I am not a religious fanatic, but I am a Christian—a born-again believer."

Kristen twisted her lips around as if she was thinking it over, pushed her tongue against her cheek, and pointed at me.

"Well, that's fine for you, just keep it to yourself, if you don't mind." Pointing to herself, she said, "I work hard while I am here, and on the weekends, I party hardy, so don't try to mix your religious convictions in with it, and we will get along just fine."

The rest of the day was filled with instructions and small talk about the work we had to do. Kristen was pleased to find my typing was very fast. She loosened up a little, and we even shared a few laughs that day.

I was still very concerned about her comments on religion, and I sensed that she had been hurt by someone who professed to know God, but that someone didn't show God or His love to her. This spiritual temporary assignment was going to be a tough one. So many times, I had found myself in situations where I wanted to cry out, "Lord, what am I doing here?" But He always came through with the right directions and answers for me to be the Creator's temporary. He chose to use me on various assignments, and I never knew what to expect next, but He was always in control, and I had to trust Him. In my prayers that night, I prayed for God to give me wisdom to be able to share my testimony with Kristen and to help her to know Jesus as I know Him.

The days passed quickly, and we received a lot of compliments about the good production in our word processing department. Hugh would come around on a regular basis to speak to us and, many times, would tell a joke that was suggestive or slightly inappropriate. At first, I blushed badly and turned my head. As months went by, when Hugh would start to tell one of his not-so-funny jokes, I would quit typing, look at him with my eyebrows raised, and softly put my hands over both ears while I had a big smile on my face. He, soon, caught on that I wasn't interested but that I wasn't going to insult him or embarrass him for his behavior. I earned his respect, and he simply stopped telling jokes around me. Kristen was aware of the changes and would laugh and talk to Hugh somewhere away from my desk.

* * * * *

Monday mornings were always difficult for Kristen. She would party all weekend, without much sleep; she would drag into the office, looking hungover and bug-eyed. One Monday, when I was feeling very chipper, she looked at me with sleepy eyes.

"What do you do on the weekends, Micki? You must sleep the whole weekend because you never seem tired or weary."

"Oh no, Kristen, I don't get a lot of sleep. I go to church!"

I took a deep breath. "We get up early, and I review my Sunday-school lesson and get my materials together for my class, then we have Sunday school at ten o'clock. I just started teaching the primaries, a class of eight-year-olds."

"Oh my goodness, how do you do it? Isn't that like working on the weekends?" She sighed.

"Oh, that's not all, that's just the start. After Sunday school, we have a wonderful praise service at church with great music and songs, then Pastor Taylor brings us the Word of God through a dynamic message."

"You mean you really enjoy that stuff, going to church and all?" she quizzed.

"I certainly do, we have great fellowship, and then, a group of us go to a restaurant and have dinner together, return to our homes and rest awhile, and back to church at seven o'clock that evening."

"What? I can't believe it. Didn't you get enough that morning?"

I laughed. "I just mean that it is the most satisfying event of my week. Have you never been to church, Kristen?"

"Oh yeah, I used to go to mass with my folks on special occasions, but I never got anything out of it. It was just a type of ritual performance. Nobody was ever any different after going, so when I got old enough to make up my mind, that's what I did—I made up my mind not to go. I could find better things to do."

I thought to myself, *Well, now, I have opened the door, and the roof didn't come crashing down on me. Thank you, Lord, for this little effort. Please, give me patience and help me to say and do the right things.*

As time passed, Kristen and I actually became good friends. We worked well together, and she knew that I gave the company the work they paid me for. Week after week, I would come in full of joy on Monday morning, and that joy would carry me all through the week. Many times, Kristen would come in sad, broken, and hurt. She would open up to me and share stories of failed love affairs, rejection, and some wild party times. She was empty, and I didn't know how I would be able to reach her. I still talked about my activities at church and my relationship with God without offending her. Once we actually got onto the subject of prayer, I was shocked when she told me she always thought you had to pay to get somebody to pray for anything that you needed. I couldn't image where she had heard that. I explained to her that God will hear a sinner's prayer, if you accept God and what Jesus has done for you; you can pray directly to the Lord, Himself, and it doesn't cost you anything because Jesus had already paid the price for our salvation. She listened, but it seemed to go in one ear and out the other. She really didn't want to talk about it.

"Kristen, don't forget you can pray anywhere, anytime. Accept Jesus into your heart, and God is always there and available. He will help you."

We had to drop the subject.

On another occasion, there was a big uproar in the area where some so-called prophet had made a declaration that Jesus was coming on a certain date. It made news in the paper and was even discussed on the television. Kristen approached me on the subject.

"Micki, did you hear all that stuff about Jesus is coming on Saturday?"

"Of course, I've heard it. Everybody is talking about it, but I know the Bible says no man knows the day or the hour, only God the Father."

Kristen cocked her head sideways and gave me a strange look. "Do you actually believe that, Micki?" She gazed into my eyes. "Don't you know that Jesus has already come?"

I thought to myself, *Oh no, what have we got into now? Where is she going with this?*

"What are you talking about Kristen? Tell me what you mean."

"My goodness." She sounded exasperated. "Of all people, I thought you would know! He's already come. Haven't you ever heard about the Virgin Mary, Joseph, and baby Jesus being born in a manger? He's already come! He was born in Bethlehem, remember, shepherds and kings, angels and all that?"

I laughed at her and at myself. "Yes, yes, Kristen, I know all about that—the birth of Jesus Christ!"

I was still laughing with relief when I continued, "But, Kristen, He is coming again!"

When I saw the look in her eyes, a chill ran through my entire body. For a moment, time was suspended in that room when I heard her say, "Nobody ever told me."

Oh my god. My thoughts overwhelmed me. *Here was a girl who had lived for thirty years in a Christian nation, around people who believed and who confessed God, that had never been told that Jesus was coming again for His children.*

"Oh, Kristen, He is coming again. Let me explain this to you."

She listened as I actually told her the wonderful plan of salvation, the soon-coming of the Lord to take us to our heavenly home, the price that Jesus paid for our sins, and His forgiveness that paves the way for all of us to be saved from an eternal hell. She listened. When I asked her if she wanted to give her life to Jesus, she quietly rejected Him.

"Well, do you think He just might come this Saturday?"

"Actually, Kristen, He could come at any time, if He does happen to come this Saturday, it will be because it is God's plan, not the prophecy of some mortal man."

"Yeah, but it is possible, right?"

"Yes, it is possible, and I will tell you what, just in case Jesus decides to come on Friday, Saturday, Sunday, or any day while I am living here in Orlando, if I go, and you don't make it, feel free to go over to my house. Get anything that you want because I won't be back. You can have my cars, food, furniture, anything, everything, okay?" I smiled.

"Oh, Micki, just be quiet. I don't want to hear anymore."

We went back to work.

When I showed up for work on Monday morning, Kristen jumped up from her desk.

"Oh, thank God," she said. "I'm so glad He didn't come."

She explained that she wasn't able to party that weekend and that she was going to try and have a better life. I knew that the Lord and I had made progress, but she wasn't there yet.

* * * * *

I had been working with Kristen for about nine months now, and she had visited in my home, and I had even been to her home a few times. She lived alone in a nice, clean mobile-home park. She had never gone to church with me, but she never complained about any witnessing that I was able to share with her.

* * * * *

It was about 5:30 p.m. on a warm spring night that I received an urgent phone call from Kristen.

"Oh, Micki, Micki!" I could hear the terror in her voice. "I need you! Something awful has happened." She was screaming. "Can you come and get me?"

"Kristen, what's wrong? Are you all right? Have you been hurt? Try to calm down. Where are you?"

She sobbed. "I'm at home, just come now, please."

"I am on my way right now, just hang in there."

I hung up the phone, grabbed my purse, and threw the car keys to my husband.

"We've got to go get Kristen. She is terrified."

When we arrived, blue lights were still flashing on the three police cars parked at her house. My heart pounded as I thought she was being arrested. When I jumped out of the car and ran to her door, Kristen grabbed me with a hug that almost stopped my breathing.

"Tell me what is wrong, what is going on here?" I looked around at the officers.

"I've got to get away from here, Micki," she said in broken sobs with tears running down her cheeks. "Will you take me home with you? I will explain everything on the way."

I looked at the policeman. "Is she free to go?"

"Yeah." He nodded. "She can go, we can handle everything else from here."

Kristen was still shaking as we got into the car. I sat in the back with her, holding her in my arms, praying and comforting her for what I still didn't know. Finally, she calmed down and started to tell me her story. She described the happening in great detail.

"I was at home, getting my stuff ready for work tomorrow when Lanny, Mae Hester's nephew, whose been staying with her for a few weeks came to my door. He's a big guy, about twenty years old but doesn't have a car, so he asked me if I could drive him to Kissimmee. I quickly told him no—that I didn't feel like going anywhere.

"He just stood there for a few minutes, wiping big drops of sweat from his head. I told him to just go find somebody else—that I couldn't do it. Then, he said, 'Okay, but would you get me a glass of water, it's hot out here.' I was aggravated, but I said I would get the water. I went to my cabinet, got a glass, and opened my refrigerator to get some cold water," she spoke with stuttered gasps.

Kristen's voice began to tremble again.

"When I closed the refrigerator and turned around, he was standing there right behind me, and...and...and..." She shook and trembled, and I could see cold sweat on her brow; violently, her body shivered with fear.

"He put a gun to my head." She sobbed.

"Oh, Kristen." My stomach lurched, and I felt a sickening feeling sweeping over me.

"What did you do?"

"I was terrified, I asked him what he was trying to pull and told him to get out of my house, or I would call the police."

He shouted and cursed at me, "No! The only place I am going is to Kissimmee, and you are going to take me."

"I told him to calm down. If it meant that much to him, sure, I would give him a ride. He told me to get in the car, which I did, and he slid in the back seat behind me while he still punched the gun into my side. I started my drive to Kissimmee which would take about forty-five minutes, but I was so afraid. I just wanted to get him out of my car and get back home.

"After about thirty minutes on the road, he told me to take a side road. When I made the turn, it soon became apparent that it was mostly deserted, as there was only a passing car every now and then. I wanted to signal to somebody but the feel of that cold steel barrel against my waist made me hesitate. The area became wooded, and the rough pavement turned into a dirt road. He ordered me to stop the car. I argued with him, asking why, but he insisted. When he told me to get out of the car, my heart just froze. He dragged me by my arm to the trunk of my car and forced me to open it. He ripped the cord off of my hair dryer and tied it around my hands. I was screaming for help, then he slapped me and gagged me with his bandanna. He found a piece of rope and made me sit down in the back seat while he tied my feet together. He shoved me down on the back seat, then he got into the front seat and started to drive my car deeper into the woods."

"Oh, Kristen." I felt tears welling up in my eyes. "What did he do to you?"

Big, silent tears were flowing down her cheeks.

"I was scared to death. I could tell by the way he was driving so slow and moaning and moving that he was fondling himself into a frenzy.

"I thought to myself, *I am going to be raped and probably murdered, but there is no one to help me. I am here, all alone, and no one can even hear my screams.* Then, I remembered you told me that God could hear me anywhere, anytime—that He would help me. So for the first time in my life, I prayed to God. I said, 'God, if it is true and that You love me, I'm sorry for the sins in my life. I don't know about life after death, but I know I am facing that kind of situation right now. Please, hear me, forgive me. If You can hear me, and You can help me, I need for You to help me now. Please, please, God, I'm sorry for the life I've lived, and I will try to do better, but please, God, help me now. Can you hear me, Lord Jesus, my God, I need you, I need you!'

"Lanny stopped the car and got out. He opened the back door and untied my feet, forcing me to walk into the woods. He took the gag off of my mouth, trying to kiss me and run his tongue down my throat. When I could, I began to talk to him. Believe it or not, suddenly, I felt a strange calmness and stopped shaking so much. I told him this was a crazy idea—that if he wanted to go out with me, why didn't he just ask? We were adults, and it didn't have to happen this way. He started to listen to me and asked me if I really meant it. By now, his passion had passed, and he found himself unable to perform any sex act. I raised my head to the stars above and whispered a soft thank you to God. I knew that God had heard me and had intervened for me. He had actually heard my prayer and protected me.

"Lanny started to calm down. His labored breathing became normal. Micki, that boy was crazy, but he was listening to me."

She started to cry harder, sobbing and shaking. She wiped her face with her hands and looked at me in such a confused, desperate way as she said, "He made me promise that I would go out with him, and then, he took me home."

"Oh, thank God, Kristen, I'm so glad you prayed, and God answered your prayer."

My heart was overwhelmed. I hugged her tight and just held her quietly for a few minutes.

"As soon as I got into my house, I called the police, then I called you."

They found the gun and ran a report for any warrants. They had been looking for him on rape charges as he was wanted in another county for raping two women and in another state for rape of a seventeen-year-old girl.

"It could have happened to me, Micki." She sobbed. "It could have happened to me."

"But it didn't, Kristen, you are all right, and he is where he will never come after you again."

My husband pulled the car into our garage, and when we were inside at the kitchen table, Kristen drank two cups of coffee and had a piece of cake. She was still filling in many of the details when she noticed my little *Bread of Life* box on the kitchen table.

"What's that?"

"Oh." I smiled, picking up the loaf-shaped box full of scripture cards. "This represents the Bread of Life, the words of Jesus from the Bible. We read one at every meal and share its meaning."

She took the box from me and pulled out a scripture card and read it.

"Behold, now is the accepted time: behold, now is the day of salvation [2 Corinthians 6:2]."

Raising her head and looking at me, she asked, "What does that mean?"

I was so happy to tell her.

One by one, she pulled and read every scripture in the box, and I explained what each one meant. When we had finished, I asked her if she had given her heart and life to a God that could hear her when she prayed. A God that could change her empty life into a wonderful relationship with Him. A God who so loved the world so much that

He sent His Son, Jesus, to save us from our sins and the corruption of this world. A God who loved her enough to die for her.

She said, "Yes, I accept Jesus."

Kristen changed her life that night, and God, soon, closed another chapter in my life as the Creator's temporary.

With a very happy heart, I waited for my next assignment.

The creation of a pure heart can be manifested by a listening friend.

2

The Wrong Place at the Right Time

It was a cold and rainy night in North Carolina as darkness crept into the world. I had no desire to go out at all. My fourteen-year-old son, Ricky, had finally finished his homework, and we got into the car to face the elements. My husband, Bill, was in the hospital for some serious tests, and I knew neither of us would be able to go to sleep unless we went to the hospital to check on him. The drive wasn't very long, but many roads would be icy in spots and dangerous. I was restless, but I still felt compelled to go. I was unaware that this was my next assignment as the Creator's temporary.

The wipers were trying to push the water from the windshield with little success. Huge puddles were filling the roads in many places. I had decided to creep along at a very slow speed. There were no other cars on the two-lane road for a while. Then, headlights beamed before me, just as I was getting ready to go around a long curve in the road. I could see in the distance that the approaching car was moving pretty fast—too fast for the curve ahead of him and us. It seemed like slow motion as I watched the car coming toward us hit the standing water and went flying into the air, off the road.

The tires on the right side of the approaching car caught the guide wires of the telephone pole and was propelled straight up to the top of the pole. I slammed on my brakes and screeched to a quick stop as I watched that car turning in the air, all four tires vertical and visible like a spaceship starting to land right in front of me. I caught my breath and came back to reality as the huge mass of steel did a back-flip, turning completely upside down while still in the air. Ricky and I screamed as we saw the body of a man fall through the rear window of the car and hit the ground. It was only with the help of God that I was able to find enough sense to get out of the way. I turned into an empty parking lot to avoid being crushed by the flying wreck as it crumbled on the road where we had been.

"Ricky, are you all right?" I panicked.

"Yes, Mom, I'm okay," he spoke in a shaky voice.

I was trembling from my head to my feet as I turned around to see his pale face in the dim light.

"Thank you, God, for protecting us. We are still alive, thank you, God." My heart was pounding so hard I could barely breathe.

My thoughts immediately turned to think about the body we saw fall from the car.

It only took a few minutes for people to be there from every-where. I really don't know where they all came from. It was like an instant, even in the cold and the rain. We sat in the car for a short time, getting our nerves together. Finally, I told Ricky I had to go and see if that man was still alive; I would need to pray with him if he was. Ricky agreed to stay in the car; he didn't want to see any more of what had happened.

I stepped out of my car and started toward the crowd, when a very kind man spoke to me, "Lady, you don't want to go over there."

"No, I really don't, sir, but can you tell me if that man is still alive?"

"Just barely, ma'am, you don't want to go over there." He urged me.

"But if he is still alive, I have to go, I just have to go, I have to pray with him."

I walked past him into the thickening crowd. The rain had lightened up a little, and more people were coming from everywhere.

I could see the shape of a body on the ground a few yards from me, when another man stopped me.

"I can't let you go over there, it's too bad," he said as he raised his hands in protest.

"Is he alive?" I questioned.

"Yes, but he is not going to make it. The ambulance is on the way, it would be better if you just stay away."

"But if he is dying, I need to pray with him. That man lying there may be facing eternity in heaven or hell. I have to go and try to pray with him."

The man stepped aside and motioned for me to pass. I walked on, praying softly.

As I knelt down beside the man, someone had covered him with a coat, so I could not see if he had injuries that were bleeding or not. He was making a gurgling sound in his throat and appeared to be semiconscious.

I asked him if he could hear me. I told him he had fallen from his car in the air, and I asked if he would like for me to pray with him.

He gurgled a sound that I took for a yes. Then, I looked around and asked, "Is there anyone here who will pray with me for this man?"

All I could hear were voices of fear and sadness.

"He's not going to make it."

"The ambulance is on the way, but he will not even be alive by the time they get here."

"Poor soul, that's just so bad, he doesn't look very old."

Again, I asked for someone to pray with me, and a kind man knelt down on the other side of the dying man and said, "I will."

I talked to the stranger lying there on the ground and asked him if he knew Jesus or wanted to know Jesus and that this would be the time to give his heart and life to him. He gurgled that he would pray with me and for me to go ahead.

I asked him to pray with me and try to repeat what I said. He gurgled a short yes.

"Dear Heavenly Father, we know that You are here with us. I ask You to come into this situation and to come into my heart."

He gurgled a long sentence that matched mine, although you could not understand what he was saying, but I knew he was praying with me.

"I ask Jesus to come into my heart... I ask You to forgive my sins and let me live... I'm sorry for my sins, and I want to live for You."

Each time, the audible gurgling matched the length of my words.

"I believe Jesus is the Son of God and that He died for me... Come into my heart, Lord Jesus, and I will serve You."

Again, he repeated with gurgling sounds. It touched my heart. I didn't know if he would live or die, but I knew he would be ready to meet Jesus if he did pass away. I paused and listened to the voices all around me.

"Crazy driver don't know when to slow down."

"Well, he's going to pay for it now, no way he is going to make it."

"Man, it's awful to just watch somebody die."

"I hear the ambulance, but if he gets in it, he will be dead on arrival, no doubt about it."

They were so negative, cruel, and uncaring that it brought a holy anger through my bones.

I reached back over to the injured man, placed my hands on his cold forehead, and prayed loud enough for all of those around me to hear.

"God, I know You just saved this man, now, oh, God, I am asking You to spare his life and heal him!"

The ambulance had arrived, and I got out of the way so they could put him on the stretcher. He immediately went into convulsions. I watched as the sirens screamed and, with lights blazing, sped down the road out of sight and into the night. The crowd dispersed as I went back to my car. I was drenched to my skin from the rain, and my first thoughts were to go back home.

"Mom, we still need to go to the hospital. Dad is waiting, and he will be worried about us."

The warm heat inside the car helped to dry my clothes and my body before we arrived at the hospital. We visited with my husband and shared our near-tragic experience. I told him about the gurgling sounds of salvation and that I felt the stranger had given his heart to the Lord. Finally, visiting hours were over, and we prepared to leave. On the elevator, Ricky looked at me and spoke quietly.

"I wonder how that man is. Do you think they brought him to this hospital?"

I said, "Probably, it's the nearest to where the accident occurred."

"Think we should go see him?" Ricky pushed the question by me.

"Well, why not?" I grinned. "After all, we are all ready at the hospital."

We made our way to the emergency room and asked about the man who was brought in earlier. He was still being treated, but his mother and sister were there. I went over to them and gently told them about the accident and that I had found the opportunity to pray with her son. Tears filled his mother's eyes as she hugged my neck and exclaimed, "I always wanted him to get saved and live right."

"I also prayed for God to touch his body and not let him die," I told her.

"Oh, honey, are you real, or are you an angel?"

I laughed and told her I was very real and introduced her to Ricky.

"I'll tell you what," I reached for paper and a pen, "give me your phone number, and I will call you in the morning and see how your son is doing."

She called it out to me, and I scribbled it down. We exchanged hugs and tears, and finally, Ricky and I were on our way home. It didn't seem so cold now, and the rain had turned into a gentle lullaby. We were exhausted.

The next morning, I found the number and called the home of the injured man; his mom answered. I explained who I was and asked about her son.

"Oh, honey." She was so excited. "You won't believe this, but he only had a few scratches—no broken bones or anything! They let him come home! He's going to be all right, and he says he is going to live for Jesus from now on. Thank you, honey, thank you for being there. Thank you for praying with my son."

"Wonderful!" I exclaimed as tears came into my eyes. "But it wasn't me. It was God, and all of the glory belongs to Him. I am just a vessel He used for that special time to intervene into the life of your son."

"And for us as well," she spoke quietly. "May God continue to use you and to bless you."

We chatted for a few more minutes, and I had to answer another call. I never even told her my name, and somehow, after that, I lost her number, so I was never able to check again. But I knew in my heart that God was at work on that cold, rainy night, when He put me at the wrong place at the right time.

I often wonder if the lady might still think that it was angels that visited her in the hospital that night. Stranger things do happen, especially in the life of the Creator's temporary. Just a normal person taking on temporary assignments in the King's service.

We can be secure in the presence of danger when following the voice of God in our hearts.

3
Runaways—Far from Home

As I answered the phone, I could hear my husband shouting.

"They are only a couple of hungry kids! They were picking oranges because they are hungry!"

"Honey, what's wrong, what's going on?"

"Oh, it's just that the old man at the store is going to call the law on a couple of kids who are hungry. He's shouting that it's illegal to pick anybody's oranges in the state of Florida without the owner's permission, and he didn't give them permission! I can't believe it, Micki, what can we do?"

"I don't know, has he called the police yet?

"Do you know these kids, how old are they?"

"Teenagers, and no, I don't know them. They are in a car, and it has an Ohio tag on it. The girl is crying, and the boy is trying to get her to get back in the car. I don't think the old man has not called the police yet, but he is really angry."

I sighed as I thought of all the things I had to do that day, then I thought of two threatened teenagers who decided to steal oranges because they were hungry, and even though they were strangers from out of state, I said, "Bring them home, if you can, and we will feed them."

It was only a matter of minutes before my husband's car pulled into our driveway, followed by a black Camaro with the teenagers. I looked out the kitchen window and watched as a slender young man opened the door for the girl. He was about six feet tall with light-brown hair, his shirt was wrinkled and open, his pants were soiled, and I could sense so much hurt in his face.

The pretty young girl got out of the car. Her long dark hair was pulled into a pony tail; she was very thin. She had on a pair of shorts and a skimpy top that matched her pink sandals. She walked with her head bent low as the young man put his arms around her shoulders.

That's somebody's daughter and somebody's son. I wonder what they are doing here? Maybe they have come to seek their fortunes at one of the big amusement parks here in Orlando, or perhaps, they have friends or relatives to visit somewhere in Florida. In any event, they appeared to be lost, and I already knew they were hungry.

As God would have it, I had put a big roast in the Crock-Pot early that Friday morning and cooked it with potatoes and vegetables. The aroma filled the house as I walked to the front door.

"Hey, there, my name is Micki, welcome to our home. Dinner is almost ready."

A smile lit up the young boy's face. "Man! That smells so good. We haven't had anything to eat in two days except a bag of chips. I'm starving."

Bill, my husband, told them to go into the bathroom and get washed up while I finished putting dinner on the table. Hot biscuits, a bowl of rice, the pot roast beaming with potatoes and vegetables plus a pitcher of sweet cold southern ice tea filled the table.

They introduced their first names as we sat down. They bowed their heads with us as Bill asked God's blessing on the food. There wasn't much conversation as the two of them filled their mouths and stomachs.

I looked at them with wonderment and compassion as I remembered the scripture, *"I was hungry, and you fed me."*

I knew the Creator's temporary was taking on a new assignment from the King of kings.

* * * *

After dinner, we sat together in the living room as they explained their dilemma to us. When we asked where they were from, I watched as the boy, Reggie, nudged his girlfriend, Susan, signaling for her not to say anything.

"Oh, we have been traveling a lot of places. We have tried to get married in Virginia, North Carolina, and Georgia. We thought we might have better luck in Florida, that's why we are here."

"What seemed to be the problem in the other states?" Bill raised his eyebrows in question to the boy, waiting for an answer.

"The truth is, Susan is only seventeen years old, and we can't get anybody to marry us without her parents' consent."

"But where are your parents, Susan?" I asked softly. She looked up at me, and I could see her eyes filling with tears.

"Oh, they wouldn't let us get married back home in—"

"Stop, Susan. It doesn't matter what they wanted. We will get married in Florida, or we will keep going until we do."

"Really, how can we do that? We are out of money, out of gas, and out of luck, Reggie."

She took a deep staggered sob.

"Well, you don't have to worry about that today, do you? How would you like to take a bath or a shower?" I tried to bring peace to the conversation.

"That would be wonderful, it seems like forever since I had a good bath." She beamed. "We haven't been using the air in the car so we could make the gas last a little longer. I know I smell stinky, and I feel gross."

I smiled at her and asked if she had some clean clothes to change into.

"We have clothes, but they are all dirty. We've been living in the car for four weeks."

Bill helped Reggie get their soiled clothes out of the car, and I loaded them into the washer as Susan got ready for her bath. Bill and Reggie chatted as they tried to figure out his plans for their future. Reggie seemed to think if he could find a job, they could start from there. He had just turned eighteen years old a few months earlier.

By the time Susan got out of her bath, a small load of their clothes had been washed and dried. I still had two full loads to finish up. She was happy to have some clean clothes to wear. Reggie pulled Susan aside and talked to her privately before he took his shower. I was sure he was instructing her not to talk about where they were from. They were running away together to start their new life, and that was all that mattered. She sat quietly, and I didn't push for information. In God's time, He would manage this situation; I knew He was in control.

It was about seven that evening when we had popcorn and drinks followed by huge bowls of ice cream. I wasn't, at all, sure how we would handle the night. We had a spare bedroom, but these kids were not married, and they were still strangers.

I was a stranger, and you took me in.

When we asked them what they wanted to do, they asked if they could make a bed and sleep in the screened lanai, our back porch, until morning; they just couldn't face another night in the car. We agreed.

* * * * *

I couldn't sleep; I was restless most of the night. Thoughts and questions kept running through my mind.

Four weeks, that's a long time. I wonder if their parents are searching for them. I'm sure they are. Could they be on the missing persons list? Will we get in trouble for harboring runaways? Some moms and dads must be worried sick, wondering where their children are. They probably imagine all kinds of things. Wrecks? Crossing paths with violent people? The possibility of being robbed or beaten up. They need to, at least, know they are still alive. It is a very mean world out there when you are young and all alone.

I know they can't stay here indefinitely, but where will they go? It's somebody's little girl. Some mother's son. How would I feel if they were my kids? Hearts must be breaking somewhere.

I prayed, "Oh, God, we need Your help. Please, guide us with Your directions and bring peace to this matter. Comfort the hearts of their parents and soften the hearts of these teenagers. Help us, Lord, to be able to reach them, to help them understand the dangers of what they are doing. This is a desperate situation that only You can handle. Give us wisdom in what we say and how we say it."

Silently praying into the wee hours of the morning, I finally found peace and drifted off to sleep.

* * * * *

The morning sun beaming into the screened Lanai porch woke them early but not before they could smell the fragrance of bacon, eggs, and pancakes. They had never eaten grits, a favorite of ours at the breakfast table, and to my delight, they found them delicious.

After breakfast, Reggie took another shower, and I found the opportunity to talk to Susan.

"Aren't you worried about what your family is thinking? Have you been in contact with them at all?"

"No, Reggie says it would only cause us more trouble because they could send the police after me to take me home. I don't want to be without him, but yes, I do worry about my mom and dad. It is probably driving them crazy."

"I'm sure it is. I would be panicked by now if my kids were missing for four weeks. Don't you think you should, at least, let them know you are all right?"

"I wish I could, but how?"

"Well, as you already know, I am a Christian, and if I could call them, I could, at least, tell them you are alive and well."

"But they would want to know where we are!"

"I wouldn't have to tell them when I call. I could tell them that you don't want them to find you and that you are trying to get married. I will tell them that you promise to call them as soon as you can, after you are married to Reggie."

"That might work, if you really promise not to tell them. Can I trust you?"

I took a deep breath, wondering how I could talk to those panic-stricken parents and not reveal where we were calling from. I knew if we used my home phone, the caller ID would show the call from the state of Florida. At least, that might help without betraying the trust Susan would put in me.

"Yes, I will keep my word. I promise I will not tell them where you are. I will only tell them that you are alive and well and that you love them."

"I do love them." She started to cry, just as Reggie walked into the room.

"What's going on here? Susan! Let's go! What have you told her?"

"Oh, Reggie, she is just going to call mom and tell her that we are okay. Micki promised not to tell them where we are. That would be okay, wouldn't it? Mom could call your mother and let her know too. They must be sick with worry by now."

"I don't think that would work." He turned and looked at me. "Did you promise not to let them know where we are or what has been happening to us?"

I looked him straight in the eyes. "I did make that promise, and I will keep it, if you will only let me make that call."

"Give me a few minutes to talk to Susan, and I will let you know, or we will just leave right now and thank you for helping us." His voice was cracking a little as he tried desperately to control his emotions.

"Sure, I'll get us a glass of tea."

They talked for about ten minutes while Bill and I discussed the situation and promises in the kitchen. I took the tea back into the living room.

"Well, what's the verdict?"

"Okay, you can make the call, but you have to keep your promise, and we will dial the number and erase it after the call."

I breathed a sigh of relief and said, "Dial the number."

Susan took the phone, dialed the number, and handed the receiver back to me. The phone was ringing, then I heard the voice of a man on the other end.

"Hello, this is Carl."

"Hello, I am calling about Susan. I want to let you know that—"

Before I could finish my sentence, he was shouting, "Wait, wait a minute, please. Cindy! Cindy! Come quick, it's about Susan."

He put his phone on speaker, and so did I.

"What? Oh, thank God. Carl, is she okay? Is she on the phone?" We could hear her running to the phone.

"Susan! Susan!" the woman screamed as she came to the phone. "Where are you, baby? Come home!"

She cried in broken sobs. I could hardly hold back the tears as I spoke.

"Susan and Reggie are here with me. They are alive and well."

"Where are they? Have they been hurt? Are they in trouble? Can we talk to her?" The woman's voice trembled as she pleaded. Susan and Reggie could hear their desperate cries.

"We are not mad at them, we're sorry for all of the confusion. They can get married here, if they will just come home. We are so sorry, Susan, Reggie, please." The voice of the brokenhearted father swept over us.

"Can they hear us? Won't you, please, talk to me, Susan? We love you, and we love Reggie too, please, talk to me. We will sign for you to get married, you can have a big wedding, whatever you want." Cindy cried.

"Oh, thank God, you are all right, we have been worried to death about you. Your mom hasn't slept a wink in weeks. It's getting the best of her. Susan, we are your parents, and we love you both, please, talk to us." Her dad was sobbing. "Reggie, your mom and dad are desperate to know that both of you are all right."

"Susan, baby, everything will be all right, and won't you forgive us and talk to us?"

There was a moment of silence, and I couldn't find any other words to say. I looked at Susan who was bawling her eyes out. Reggie was trying to comfort her as big tears slid down his cheeks. I held the receiver up in the air, and Susan took it.

"Mama." She was weeping. "Mama, Daddy, I love you too."

Precious moments followed as Susan and Reggie talked to her parents who promised to give them permission to marry. Reggie told them where they were. Carl said he would take the next flight out to Orlando, if they would pick him up at the airport. He would buy the gas and drive them back to Ohio while they planned their wedding.

Everyone was crying tears of joy and relief. My heart felt as light as a feather as I praised God for taking over the phone call and the situation.

Around four o'clock, Bill gave them money for gas and snacks at the airport. It was the last we saw of Susan and Reggie as they excitedly went to the airport to meet and pick up her dad.

Still, today, when I pick up an orange, I take a moment and hold it in my hands as the memory of Susan and Reggie crosses my mind. Quietly and with a thankful heart, I think about the precious moments God has blessed me with as I surrender to His will—the unforgettable way He can use a willing vessel for His purpose. We are His hands extended to a lost and dying world.

I eagerly wait for my next surprise assignment as the Creator's temporary.

After facing the storms of life, the sun shines so much brighter.

4

Where, Oh, Where Can She Be?

Her name was Daisy, a middle-aged woman with bright-blue eyes and soft white hair that framed her weathered face. A mother of six children, and some of them are grown up with their own children. A house full of rough-and-ready kids and grandkids who enjoyed every moment spent together, especially at Grandma Daisy's house.

I met her one Saturday afternoon while we were visiting different homes in a small neighborhood. A group of us, on visitation for our church, ended up in this hillside village which some people called "The Turkey Ring." Large framed houses very close together on a street winding around in a big circle. Everybody knew everybody on that street, as most of them had grown up together and had lived there for years. There were plenty of children playing in the streets as mothers and grandmothers sat on the front porches, talking and laughing together.

It looked like most of the men just hung out at the house with a homemade garage. Five cars parked there, needed to be worked on; two with hoods raised and a few men discussing the best way to make that old car run.

When I went into the dirt yard at Grandma Daisy's house, several kids scampered inside to let her know that some strangers were coming. Daisy came to the door wearing a big white apron and, wiping her hands on it to clean the grease from her fingers.

"Hey," she shouted to us, "I've been cooking chicken, are y'all hungry?"

She had never met a stranger, and the sweetness in her voice was refreshing.

"No, thank you, we're just in the neighborhood to invite you and your family to our church."

"Where's your church at?" She smiled broadly, showing a mouth full of crooked teeth. "It's kinda hard for me to get up and get all of these kids ready for church on a Sunday morning."

"Oh, our church is Soul's Harbor, down on Big Creek Rd, do you know where it is?"

"Oh, sure, y'all just got a new preacher, didn't ya?"

"We did, and we want to get that church filled up with some of these friendly people in the surrounding neighborhood."

"Well, that's good. I don't drive anymore, and it would take a couple of cars to get all of my crowd to a church."

"Well, we have some good news for you, Mrs.... Uh, what is your name?"

"Oh, just call me Daisy, that's what everybody calls me."

"Daisy, the good news is we have a bus at our church now, and we will be driving right past your house every Sunday, and we would love to give you and your family a ride to church."

"Is that right? Nobody ever brought a bus to the Turkey Ring before. That sounds really good."

Two little boys tugged at her apron. "Can we go, Grandma Daisy? Can we go?"

She reached down and patted them on the head and motioned for them not to interrupt, but they were persistent.

"We could all ride in the bus, Grandma Daisy. They are gonna be coming by here anyway."

"Okay, boys, we will think about it. Now, y'all get on out there and play. These ladies came to visit me not all of you, young'uns."

The boys scampered off to play, and Daisy invited us to take a seat in the rocking chairs on her front porch. We sat down to talk with her for a little while longer. It was just like we had always known each other. The comfort of her southern conversations; the twinkle in her blue eyes. She was probably about fifty years old but looked ruggedly to be in her late sixties. You could tell the family was poor, but they were so happy and relaxed, it was a pleasure just to be around them. It was around 1967 when we met; a time when people really talked and laughed with each other. Neighbors were real neighbors, lending a hand when needed and watching out for each other. A quieter time before cell phones and the internet took over conversations.

* * * * *

My friend, Faye, and I stayed longer than we had planned, and I enjoyed sharing the laid-back life they had. Daisy promised that Sunday morning, she would be waiting with, at least, four of the kids to go to church with us. She was true to her word.

The Bagwells became a big part of our congregation as the church continued to grow. Daisy was faithful to be waiting when the bus arrived each and every Sunday morning. I have to admit that when we had an old-fashioned dinner at the church, Daisy always brought the best food. We became very good friends, and in our conversations, she would talk about the kids and how so many of them had grown up so fast. Sometimes, during our conversations, she would pause with a faraway look in her eyes. I wondered if something could be bothering her. She seemed happy and jolly most of the time, but then, I could sense sadness deep down inside of her.

One Saturday afternoon, she brought a gallon of blackberries over to my house. She said she had been out with the children, picking them all morning, and she planned on making me a blackberry sunker. I wasn't sure what a sunker was, but she exclaimed it was a family pie of sorts, and something similar to a cobbler. It would be delicious hot with ice cream on top. She had brought me extra blackberries to enjoy by themselves or anyway I might want to fix them. I was happy for the fresh blackberries, and my mouth watered, thinking about the sunker I would soon enjoy. Frank, her husband, had dropped her off and would be back in about an hour, so we had plenty of time for conversations without all of the children running around. The pleasure was all mine.

We laughed and talked about so many different things, then I noticed she grew quiet and had that faraway look in her eyes again.

"What's on your mind, Daisy? You seem to have drifted away for a while."

"Oh, it's really nothing—not really anything anybody can do anything about."

"Do you want to tell me about it? Is something wrong?"

"Oh, I don't want to worry you with it, actually, it's about one of my girls. I have a daughter that I have never told you about."

"You do? Does she live out of town or something?"

"Well, to tell you the truth, I don't know where she lives. I haven't heard from her in fifteen years."

"What? That's a long time. Did you two have a quarrel or something? Don't you think there is a way you could make up? I know you must miss your daughter."

"Oh, I wonder about her all of the time, and sometimes, at night, after everybody else is sleeping, I cry for her. Nobody has seen her or heard from her since she ran away."

"How old was she when she left you? Is it possible that she was taken?"

"Humph! She was taken, all right—taken right out of her mind and out of our lives by a smooth-talking salesman that showed up at our house one day."

"A salesman?"

"Yes, he was smooth as honey dripping out of the comb, he was a looker too, and when he saw that Nancy was a pretty young thing, he set his mind on getting her. She had just turned fifteen, but I guess she looked about eighteen to him. He was probably at least twenty-five, and he hung around the village for about a week. Nancy thought he was a gift from God, but he was more likely the devil in disguise."

"Oh no. What happened?"

"It was the first week of school, and I waved bye to Nancy as she got on the school bus and left. She should have been home on that same school bus about four o'clock, but she didn't get off. I thought she had missed the bus, so we started asking some of the other teens in the neighborhood if they knew where she was. The story they told was that right after the bus left the village, Nancy told the driver that she felt sick and wanted off the bus. She said she was going to walk back to the house. Most of them didn't think anything about it, but one boy said he saw that salesman sitting in his car down at the end of a side road."

"My goodness, did they see her get in the car?"

"Yes, one of the girls at the back of the bus happened to look back just in time to see Nancy go over to the car and get in. She figured Nancy was just up to having some fun, so she didn't tell anybody about it."

"Did you know the name of the salesman or the company he was working for?"

"No, he just said his name was Joe. We found out who he was working for, and they said he called in that day and said he was quitting, going to California or somewhere."

"Did you call the police and report her missing?"

"We sure did, and we put out posters and everything, but nothing ever turned up. That was fifteen years ago. Nobody knows where she is. We don't even know if she is dead or alive. I just try to put it out of my mind as much as I can, but it ain't easy."

I reached over and gave her a comforting hug, then I looked deep into her sad blue eyes.

"Daisy, you need closure on this situation, and I know someone who knows exactly where Nancy is."

"Whaaat? How could you? I mean what are you talking about?" She gasped.

"I am talking about God. He knows everything, Daisy, He knows what has happened since that day, fifteen years ago. He knows if she is still alive and where she is right now."

"I've prayed about it, but I just never thought about it that way, Micki."

"I am sure that He knows the answers to your problems, and we might not be able to fix things, but He sure can. He can give you peace. He can perform miracles today, just like He had in the past. You do believe in a miracle-working God, don't you, Daisy? You are His child, and He wants to help you. That is why you are here with me right now."

"Do you really think God would pay attention to my heartache and let me know what happened to my little girl? I ain't nothing special, you know."

"Daisy, God loves you, and He loves Nancy too. The Bible says, *with God, all things are possible.* Do you believe that, Daisy? Do you believe that God knows what has happened to Nancy?"

She spoke in a broken voice, just above a whisper, "I do, I really do."

"God says that if two or more people ask anything in the name of Jesus, believing He will do it, we just have to have faith believing and not doubting. You and me make two, Daisy, and Jesus says He is here in the midst of us. Can we ask Him for help now?"

She grabbed my hands and held them tight, bowed her head, and said, "Let's ask Him!"

We started to pray, and I could feel the presence of the Lord. Daisy was praying as hard as I was. Tears filled our eyes, and a great burden was lifted off of our hearts. I knew I had just encountered another assignment as the Creator's temporary. When we finished praying and wiping the tears from our eyes, we began to laugh with joy.

"Nancy's birthday is in two weeks, and I believe I will know something about her by then."

"Keep the faith, Daisy. Remember, God is able."

* * * * *

All through the following two weeks, I held hope and believed that the answer would come before Nancy's birthday. I knew that my assignment was to meet Daisy and give her the opportunity to know God. She had given her heart and life to Jesus and served Him every day. She had been given inspiration to build her faith, to give her hope and peace.

* * * * *

I heard a car pull into the drive about eight o'clock that Saturday morning, and I wondered who would be coming to my house that early. When I opened the door, there stood Daisy beaming the biggest smile I had ever seen; standing beside her was a young woman and a little boy.

"Micki, I want you to meet my daughter. This is Nancy! And this cute will fellow is Curtis. He's my grandson."

My mouth dropped open, and I smiled as big as Daisy.

"Thank God, thank God! Come on in, Nancy, it is so good to meet you."

During the next hour, we talked about everything and everywhere that Nancy had been. She admitted that she always wanted to write home, and during the past five years, after Curtis was born, she had tried on several occasions but would tear up the letter and throw it away. Every time she looked into the bright-blue eyes of Curtis, she would see her mother's bright-blue eyes. She knew she had left the wrong way; she felt everyone would be angry with her and try to press charges against her husband, Joe, so for years, she didn't make any attempt to get in touch. Lately, she had been thinking more and more about coming home from Texas. She explained that for the last two weeks, there was a burning sensation in her chest that she just couldn't shake. She had talked it over with Joe, and they agreed that it was time for her to return for a visit.

I knew it wasn't really her time; it was God's time! Daisy found peace, and God gets all of the glory. He had found a way to put me and Daisy together so that we could pray and ask for His favor in this situation. God needs people who are willing to do His will without hesitation, step out in faith, and open the windows of heaven to a hurting world. He is the Creator, He does know everything, and there are no secrets from Him. He just needs to use us individually while we are here on this Earth, on assignment in a hurting world as the Creator's temporary on a job for the King of kings, Lord Jesus. Praise His holy name.

When you pray, you can overcome doubt by true faith. You only have to truly believe.

5

But God!

She snuggled close to him to try and get warm; the night was chilly and damp. He reached over and covered her with his big arms and crossed a leg over her legs to give more body heat.

"I'm so cold," she said as a shiver shook her body. "What are we going to do? I'm freezing out here."

"I don't know, Tess, I wish I had some answers. Here take more of my blanket." He pushed more of the light blanket over to her. "Does the ground seem to be getting wet?" He sat up on one elbow. "Oh lord." His voice was weak. "It is starting to rain."

They were sleeping on the ground at a deserted park.

It was early November, and she thought of all the people who would start shopping and begin to put up their Christmas lights and decorations. Her thoughts went back to a time when they had a three-bedroom brick home with shining Christmas lights and presents under the tree. She remembered the kids celebrating their holiday; Nevada, her six-year-old daughter who lived with them; her son, Eli, who stayed with his dad in North Carolina, came to spend the Christmas week with her; and JJ's three children, Hannah, Jake, and Tim. She wondered what they were doing tonight. *At least, they are warm, and they are not hungry.* Those thoughts became her only consolation. She was hungry; living off of crackers and soda didn't allow her to have much strength. She was brought back to realization as water seeped under her body.

"What did you say? Yes, it is raining, we've got to find some shelter!"

They crawled out onto the wet ground, wrapping their blankets in a roll to help keep them dry, and began to run for a covered gym set at the park. Crouching down close together, they could hear the pounding rain hitting the top of the metal covering while it was blowing on their faces. When the rain slacked up a little, they ran toward the all-night grocery store just down the street.

They knew they would not be welcome to go in, so they ran behind the building. They gathered up some of the wooden pallets and laid them on the pavement. Finding large sheets of cardboard was easy, and it made a sheltered top for them by pushing it against a tree and stabilizing it against the building. It kept the rain off of them, but they were shivering from the cold and being wet.

"Well, I can't take this anymore. I have got to do something, JJ. Can't we just try to go inside to get a little warm?" she spoke with trembling lips as her body shivered.

"I guess we can try, Tess, all they can do is run us off."

"Or maybe call the police?" she questioned.

"We haven't done anything for them to call the law," he protested. "Let's make a run for it, head for the restrooms. It will be warm in there."

Inside the ladies' restroom, Tess pulled off her wet jacket and shirt. She held them up to the noisy hand dryer. The heat felt wonderful, and as she warmed her hands, she held them to her face. Finally shaking her hair dry in front of the dryer, she began to quit shivering and started to grow warm and slightly comfortable. She wanted to lie down on the floor and sleep until daylight, but she knew other people would be coming in, and she had to find JJ.

JJ had dried off as much as he could with the dryer, but then, he walked into the store, looking around and filling his pockets with small food items.

We can, at least, have something to eat when we go back outside, he thought as he crammed small cakes, chips, and a jar of peanut butter into his jacket. *We just can't go on living like this.*

* * * * *

The rain had gotten lighter, and the handmade shelter gave them enough comfort to stay dry and to fall asleep again. At sunrise, they tore the shelter apart as much as they could and headed back to the park. They knew of places for the homeless to be sheltered and fed, but they would have to split up, and neither of them wanted to be apart.

"JJ, where do we go from here? We have been living this survival thing for about seven months now. The spring and summer wasn't so bad, but I don't think I will make it through the winter." Tess started to cry.

"I will find a way. I love you, and I am so sorry that we have had to live like this, Tess. I know it is my fault, and I shouldn't have dragged you into this situation."

JJ looked down and shuffled his feet in the dirt.

"Well, you didn't force me, JJ. I wanted to get high and get numb too. It was the only way I could take what we were facing. Your dad passing away and, then, having to move from our rental house because it was sold out from under us. It just wasn't right. I know we handled it wrong, but what else was there to do?"

Talking together on a park bench, they weighed their pros and cons, and JJ came up with a possible solution.

"You remember that girl, Ginger, that lived with her parents on Mom's street?"

"Yes, I remember her, she stays strung out on meth more than we did. What about her?" Tess asked with raised eyebrows.

JJ managed a smile. "Well, you know she was staying there with her mom before her mom passed away. Now, the house is in some kind of legal dispute. I heard the house is empty, and she may inherit the property. There is no power, water, or heat, but just maybe, if we play our cards right, she would let us stay there. We could watch out for the place."

"Yeah, but what would she want in return?" Tess quizzed. "People don't do anything for nothing, and she would want something out of us."

"I've got it, Tess. She needs meth, and I know how to get it for her. We will work out an exchange. A place to stay for a while, and there is a fireplace in the garage where they built their den. It might just work. What do you think?"

"Anyway, we could give it a shot. We don't have anything to lose, and it would get us out of the weather. We can go to the food bank and get food too. She would probably go for it."

They started the four-mile trek back to the neighborhood where Ginger lived.

Ginger was surprised to see them, but since JJ had always been a friend, she agreed to go along with the deal. They would have to stay in the garage that had been converted into a den, get their own firewood, and take care of the place. The rest of the house was off limits, and if anyone else showed up, they couldn't go to the door or let anyone know they were staying there. It would only be temporary, and oh yes, they had to figure out a way to get the meth and drugs that she needed. The deal was closed.

Carrying what few belongings they had left, Tess and JJ set up a place to stay in the dark garage. Both of them combed the surrounding wooded area for any wood to start a fire. Carrying armloads of wood and making many trips, they finally had enough to keep a good fire in the fireplace going through the night. They slept soundly and warm for that first night but woke up to a freezing-cold room the next morning. The fire had gone out.

* * * * *

For weeks, through the cold winter months, they searched for wood to burn. One of the neighbors had a fence that was broken and falling down; they took wood from it too. They burned anything they could find in the fireplace. They went through the trashcans in the neighborhood, gathering plastic milk bottles and used the spigot in the yard at JJ's mom's house to fill the jugs with water to drink and take baths. Their faces, hair, and bodies were darkened with soot, and they smelled of wood smoke, but it was working. JJ's mom actually lived with her daughter, JJ's sister, about half a mile down the road. After a family fight, JJ's sister had taken out restraining orders through the police to keep them off the property. However, when no one else was there, JJ's mom would prepare some food for them and let them take a real bath and wash their hair, but it didn't happen very often. She gave JJ a small propane heater so he and Tess could cook some food in the garage. Things seemed to be better, but when JJ picked up drugs for Ginger, he also picked up drugs for himself and Tess. Their lives consisted of sleeping almost all of the time, using drugs, getting high, and then, the hallucinations started. It was like crazy things were happening, especially to JJ. Tess held back and would not give in to the things they were imagining. JJ would scream that he could see the shadow people all around him. He would ask Tess if she could see them.

"No! No!" Tess would cover her ears, close her eyes, and scream out, "They are just demons, JJ, demons, and I plead the blood of Jesus." She was high too, but in her conscience somewhere, the name of Jesus had evolved as a call for help against the powers of darkness. The room would grow deathly cold.

"We are in hell!" JJ screamed as loud as he could. "Everybody thinks hell is hot, but no, no, hell is cold and filled with evil spirits, and I can see them, I can feel them. Watch out, Tess. They are coming to get you. Hey! Hey! You leave her alone!" He stumbled around the room, grabbing at the things he thought he saw.

Tess was terrified. There was no more sleeping until they passed out. After a while, things were so scary on drugs, they were fighting demons, seeing all kinds of horrible things, and sleep left them; they couldn't even pass out anymore for the tormenting they had to endure. They did not sleep, at all, for forty-five days and nights. They were stoned out of their minds. After the fall of a heavy snow, one night, a drift piled up against the door. When they tried to get out, they had to dig their way to clear a path. JJ looked at Tess and reminded her that if they had still been sleeping in the woods, they would both be dead by now. Tess whimpered as she muttered, "I know." Somehow, even the terrible situation they were living in still seemed better than death.

In the meantime, Ginger had been arrested and had to stay in jail for thirty days. When she served her time, she came back to the house. Immediately, she went into a rage; the place was wrecked. She threw them out. They were homeless again.

JJ had to be in court by 9:00 a.m. the day she threw them out of her house. He was a mess but begged her to take him to the court house. She refused, and he could not find a way to get there. All of their so-called friends had forsaken them. Their families wanted nothing to do with them anymore. No mercy could be found, but God had not forgotten them. They had walked a few miles in the freezing weather when JJ collapsed and fell down. His face looked so pale against the cold ground. Tears in the dirt became mud against his cold face as he cried in a whimpering voice.

"Okay, God." He wept. "Okay, God, if You are out there some-where, just let me die. I can't go on anymore. This is the end, please, God, help me or let me die." His face fell into the mud again.

Tess was crying. They were more sober now; realization of their awaiting fate was creeping into their wretched minds.

"Get up, JJ, you can't lie there, get up! You will freeze to death if you don't get up!" Tess tugged at his jacket and gently kicked against his hip. "Get up." She pleaded, "Oh, God, help me. How did we get into all of this mess? I don't want JJ to die, and I don't want to die. What can we do? I want to change my life, we just need some help, God. Please, tell me what to do."

Tess was on her knees, violently shaking JJ. "Come on, get up, we will get some help." Tess bent down over his body, burying her head onto his back, and wept uncontrollably. "I guess we are both going to die here." Fear gripped her like a huge snake wrapping itself all around her body. The horrible memories of the past year flooded her mind—thoughts of her alcoholic mom and a daddy that told her she would never amount to anything. She felt as if she didn't deserve to live.

After her first marriage and two beautiful children had ended in divorce, she decided to really live on the wild side of life for a while. After she moved in with JJ, things began to change again. They had enjoyed good jobs and a family. They didn't do drugs, and she thought they had beaten their old habit. It wasn't until old friends started coming around that she began to doubt JJ. While she was working, he entertained a lot of old buddies, and she soon discovered he was back to his old habit of using meth. He had become ill and aggravated, fussing and accusing her. Things got worse, and fights erupted between them. Smashing things in their home, ruining their furniture, and scaring Nevada who would run and hide. He had gone crazy on a few occasions. He tried to commit suicide, and she rescued him, even though he had thrown knives at her and used an axe to try to get into the door. Through it all, she knew he loved her in spite of himself, and she loved him and needed him. He had tried to do better, but the drugs and meth just ruined everything in their lives, and now, they were dying. The fear of the unknown, imagining flames of hell tormenting them, and a God she could no longer face filled her heart with terror. Her thoughts were broken as she heard the sound of a car stopping in the road beside of them.

A young man rolled down the window and yelled, "Hey, what's going on? Is everything okay? Do I need to call 911 for you?"

Tess jumped up and went to the car. "No, he's just sick. Can I use your phone? I need to call someone to come and get us, please."

"Yeah, okay, here's my phone, but he looks like he might need to go to the hospital."

"It's all right." Tess calmed down and dialed a number. "We will be all right." She called me and asked if I would let them come over and see Nevada for a while.

On the phone with me that dreadful night, Tess didn't dare tell me of their situation. She told me where to find them, saying they would meet me at the end of the road. I could hear the pleading in her voice, and I knew they were in trouble, so I said I would come. She handed the young man his phone, and he drove away.

"JJ, don't die, we are getting help. Micki is on her way. I told her we want to see Nevada."

* * * * *

The situation was strange, to say the least. Tess had, at one time, been married to my grandson, Jeff. After the birth of their two children, Eli and Nevada, they had split up. Eli was with Jeff, and Nevada was with Tess. I was living in Florida at the time all of the trouble started. Bill had passed away as you will see in another story, and I was married to Charles Carpenter.

I remember the day the phone rang, and I heard the news that Tess had been arrested and was in jail. Nevada, who was seven years old, had been taken to JJ's mother's home for temporary guardianship. JJ's mom had a good heart but with a house already full of people; it just couldn't be the place for Nevada. Of course, Nevada knew the family, but since Tess and JJ had never married, they were not blood relatives. I was afraid that the arrangement wouldn't last long, and Nevada might be put into the court systems and sent anywhere. I was Nevada's great-grandmother; I was a blood relative. She couldn't leave the state of South Carolina at that time. I had to do something. I made plans immediately to get back to South Carolina. My sister lived there, and I could stay with her while I worked things out. Charles understood the urgency of the situation, and I was on my way. It took a few weeks, but soon, I was awarded temporary custody, and Nevada was placed with me. My life changed abruptly.

I found a house, and Charles packed up our things and moved to South Carolina to be with us. I knew I was asking a lot of him since we were planning our retirement in Florida and had only been back there for three months. He was a good man—a Christian—and he knew and loved Nevada. He was willing to make the change. I thank God for him every day.

I enrolled Nevada in school and took on the role God had planned for us. I had seen Tess on several occasions when she wanted to see Nevada. I could have been mad, resistant, and mean for all the hurt and trouble she had brought into our lives. I could have brushed my hands and heart of her, but God doesn't work that way, does He? Even after everything that had happened, I still felt compassion and mercy for Tess who was once like my granddaughter. I couldn't let it go; I knew she was suffering, doing drugs, and miserable. She was hurting, and I had her little girl.

We would meet at a fast-food restaurant, the park, or public places so they could visit for a few hours at a time. After a while, JJ would come and visit too, and I became more acquainted with him. The only comfort I could give them was to help with some food or transportation. Although my husband knew Tess, he did not know JJ at all, and there was no way he would allow them to visit in our home.

"Druggies, thieves—we will not allow them to come in here and take what little we have," he grumbled. "How can you even care after the way they treated Jeff, anyway?"

We had to meet somewhere else.

During those months, Tess and JJ spent some days in women's shelters and detox facilities. When in the shelters, they managed to find a job here and there, and then, they would leave those places and those jobs. I knew about the days they were having to sleep in the park or anywhere they could find. When the weather began to grow cold, I gave them blankets and also took them food from time to time. Every night, I prayed for them, earnestly begging God to change their lives for their sakes, and for Nevada and Eli as well. Nevada was a precious little girl with big blue eyes and curly brown hair. It was so difficult for her to understand the change.

"Why can't Mommy come here?" she begged.

"I want to see JJ.

"Why can't I go home?

"When will mommy come and get me?" Many questions filled her mind and broke my heart.

"Let's keep praying about it, honey."

At night, she said her prayers, and sometimes, she cried herself to sleep. For the first time in my life, I was at loss for answers. I had a lot of questions of my own. I was very glad when I knew Tess and JJ were staying in Ginger's house, but they were about twenty miles away, and I did not see them much. I hoped everything was going better for them.

The night that Tess called me in a panic about JJ, I had picked them up and took them to a motel, which my sister and I paid for. They were able to stay there, take showers, sleep, eat, and get their acts together for a few days. I took Nevada to spend some time with them; all visits had to be supervised by me. I drove them around to various shelters to try and help them find a place to live and get better. Tess moved into the women's shelter, and JJ moved into the one next door for men. They were separated, but when they had to catch the bus in the mornings to look for work, they would meet downtown for a while. Both of them managed to find jobs, stay clean, and make a little money. We shared a great time at our home for a festive thanksgiving dinner. The atmosphere was like one big happy family. Things were getting better. Charles had allowed them to visit in our home. I knew that God was working on His plan for all of us.

Since the Christmas holiday was just a month away, we decided to do some early Christmas shopping together. On the way back to the shelters, a car made an illegal left turn in front of me, and I couldn't avoid hitting the car broadside. Tess was in the front passenger seat beside of me, and Nevada was in the backseat with JJ. We were wearing our seat belts, but JJ reached over to Nevada to restrain her from getting hurt. He hit his head hard on the head rest of the front seat. He had a concussion. Tess was in the right passenger seat in the front, and the impact jammed her neck and back. I had slight injuries to my neck, back, and to my hand, but none of us had to be hospitalized. I thanked God that He had protected us from serious injury. Both cars had to be towed in, and the ambulance took the three of them to the hospital. I stayed with the police and waited for the wrecker and Charles to pick me up, then I went to the hospital to be checked out. The woman who was driving the other car was shaken but uninjured. We were at the hospital all night.

Within a week, the insurance company of the car at fault offered a settlement to Tess and JJ. They accepted it on the spot. I decided to wait until my injuries were over before I would settle. Tess and JJ managed to buy Christmas presents for the kids and also an old used car with the money from their settlement. Then, the money was gone.

Now that they had the car, that became their dwelling place. I remember hearing JJ say they would never be homeless again because, now, they could sleep in the car. That is exactly what they tried to do wherever they could find a place to park it. Many times, the police would wake them up and send them on their way. Eventually, they began to park the car in our driveway to sleep. Nevada managed to soften up Charles with her pleading and was allowing them to do this.

Nevada wanted her mom to sleep in the house with her. They still were not married, so in time, Tess moved into Nevada's bedroom while JJ still slept in his car in the driveway.

I invited them to go to church with all of us on Sunday. At first, there were excuses like not having the right clothes to wear. We believed that all of the family should go to church together, and our home was locked and unoccupied while we were gone to church. Finally, out of obligation to us and some heartfelt appreciation, they agreed to go.

Our church was a friendly place, and they felt welcome. We had fellowship dinners on Wednesday nights, and they would join us for fellowship and food. In time, they were going to church with us for their own reasons. They began to listen to the message; they knew that God had reached way down for them, and they were thankful for not dying in their hours of darkness. Soon, they found their way to an altar of forgiveness and really started to turn their lives around.

They were not allowed to live as man and wife in our home, and I encouraged them to get married and do the right thing.

Christmas came, and we allowed Tess and JJ to have Christmas with all of their children in our house. It was a time of warmth, fellowship, and a loving family. JJ's three children came for the celebration, and Eli came down from North Carolina to stay with us for a week. The New Year was looking brighter.

They were determined to go into rehab, change their lives completely with God's help, and rebuild their family life.

The pastor took a special interest in them. The church family played a great part in helping them build confidence in what they could do through God's power. The DSS worker who made regular visits to our home to see them began to notice the difference as we witnessed to her and shared their testimonies.

* * * * *

On December 27, 2015 they were married in our church. Their church wedding was beautiful, and all five of their children participated in the wedding.

Shortly after the wedding, JJ also moved into our home. They had started to make great changes in the way they thought, in the music they listened to, and the shows they watched on the television. They had forsaken all of their old ways and their old friends. Life was new to them. They read their Bibles at home and prayed to God every night. They were baptized in our church.

In May, they both enrolled in a wonderful rehab in Greenwood, South Carolina. It was called Faith Home. They stayed committed. They fought the fight, stayed the course, graduated, and changed their lives for good. Although their graduation was in a city about seventy miles from home, my sister, her husband, Nevada, and myself, along with JJ's mom and his daughter, Hannah, made the trip to the graduation. We were happy when their social worker and one of her friends showed up as well. We were all so proud of them.

After their return to our home and to our church, Trinity West, they joined in all of the activities and shared their testimonies of God's deliverance. Only three days after coming home, a man in our church recommended JJ to a friend of his who owned a painting company. He explained about their past life and the present life they now had. The owner was a Christian and wanted to help. He hired JJ for the commercial and industrial painting job and was proud of the work he did. Tess found a part-time job in a local fast-food place, and she was still able to be home with Nevada after school. She took care of Nevada's clothes, dressed her in the mornings, fed her, and helped get her off to school. After school, she would give her a snack and help with her homework. She was a caring and loving mother to Nevada once again. Both JJ and Tess were great helpers around the house. Tess enjoyed cooking again, and she was an excellent house-keeper. JJ cut the grass, trimmed the hedges, helped clean the gutters, and fixed things around our home. He and Charles were getting along great now.

The church helped them with so many of their needs, including a better and safer car to drive. The social worker from the department of social services commented that she too felt like it was time for unsupervised visitations, so they were able to take Nevada out on their own. She and I both agreed that it would not be very long before Nevada would be living in the apartment with them after their move.

Tess and JJ continued to grow in the church. One Sunday, they practically filled a pew with all three of JJ's children and Nevada sitting beside of them. They participated in a discipleship class. JJ and Tess felt the need to minister their testimony and the message of God to others. Some of the people in our church have been amazed at their growth, commenting that even the countenance of Tess and JJ had changed. Who knows, the great Creator may also give them some temporary assignments to help build His kingdom. JJ had already began witnessing on his job.

I thought I was sent on assignment to help Nevada when I took the call to move back to South Carolina, but now, I know I was sent here for JJ and Tess as well.

I heard a story once about how the mother eagle trained her little eaglets. She would take them from the nest and drop them so that they would free fall through the air. If they didn't learn to fly, she would swoop under them, catch them, and take them back to the nest, then she would continue to drop them and catch them, until they could soar on their own.

At church, one Sunday night, as Tess and JJ were praying at the altar, I stood back and noticed how the church family gathered around them, praying with them, hugging and showing such love to them. It seemed as if I was watching a page turning in the restoration of their life. I felt a warm glow of satisfaction inside of me when I felt sure that, now, they could fly; they were strong enough to stand on their own and move on with the life that God had ordained for them.

When they moved out of our home into a home of their own, they continued to work on their jobs, and Tess got a raise and a promotion. JJ has already started witnessing to many of his coworkers. The people of Trinity Church West showed their loving care and true Christian spirit by blessing them with furniture and household goods to get into their new apartment. God's amazing grace and mercy brought many wonderful miracles to unfold before their eyes. Nevada loves being with them again, and although I knew I would be saddened when she left us, I was also content to know that she would be brought up by Christian parents who love the Lord. Today, JJ's mom came to church with him. God had restored all things and even more than what they had before.

An even more amazing event took place after Tess regained custody of Nevada. Because she had proven herself to the department of social services by such a dedicated change, she received news that, now, Eli would be coming to live with them in South Carolina for a while. Her heart was filled to the brim with love and appreciation for the miracles God had worked in her life. Eli arrived in time for the Christmas holidays in December 2016. Looking back over all of the events that took place, I can truly say that the year of 2016 had been an amazing display of the grace of a loving God. Where death was facing them, a devil determined to destroy them could have meant the end of everything for them, but God made the difference, changed lives, and restored health and happiness.

It has been almost two years now, and sadly, I must say that when Tess and JJ got out on their own, even though they had both children in their home, they quitted attending church and, in their weakness, failed to resist the temptations of the devil. They eventually turned their backs on God and fell back into the horrible habit doing meth. They were in denial and wanted nothing to do with me or the people from the church anymore. As the habit grew, they began to steal to have money to buy drugs. There were lots of arguments and fights. Once, JJ tried to choke Tess, and she had the police pick him up. Both of them ended up on probation and tried to do better for a while. They ended up with nothing again. JJ and Tess split, and he ended up serving some time in prison.

Tess got her second chance, and Nevada lives with her. Eli returned to live with his family in North Carolina, but he would visit Tess on occasions. Nevada will be thirteen years old this year. JJ just recently got out of prison, and Tess had asked him for a divorce. She is drug free and a good mother to Nevada. She is working and going to college to be a social worker. Her desire is to help other people in desperate situations. Tess has acknowledged that the only answer to the world today is God's love. It is my sincere prayer that the things they learned and cherished while serving God will keep them in God's graces. God can definitely bring about change, but it is up to the individual to choose God's forgiveness and His way. Jesus Christ is the way, the truth, and the life. You have the choice, and choices have consequences. There is always hope in Jesus Christ. He paid the price for our salvation at Calvary.

God is not mocked; whatever you sow in this life is what you will reap. Remember, when you are committed to serving God, you will find that He that is in you is greater than he that is in the world. What God does for any of His children, He will do for you if you will just open your heart to serve Him, put the past behind you, and move forward into His loving care. Many people out there need someone to show them the way, lend a hand, to bring hope to those who have given up hope. To point them to God and the answers they are seeking. We are not laying up treasures here in this world, but great is your reward in heaven.

Being in the service of the King of kings on temporary assignment for the Creator is not always an easy path; sometimes, it is a trail of tears and heartaches, but it is worth it all. We can participate in God's plans, watch them unfold, and see His miracles working as He still changes lives today. He is currently searching for volunteers! How about you?

When the world is dark, and the road is rough, the light to Jesus shines on your pathway.

6

Where Is God?

Donnie was a precious child—loving and kind. He smiled at everybody and had a very good nature. As a young boy, he avoided troubles and fighting at school and in the neighborhood. As a teenager, he gave his heart and life to God as he accepted Jesus as his Savior. Many times, he was seen at the altar with his arms raised high, praising the Lord. He helped in Christmas plays, children's crusades, Royal Rangers, and various ministries. He was always available and anxious to help in any way that he could. He grew into a kind and loving person in his manhood. Everyone cared about Donnie. He was special—different from most people in his dedication. As all young men do, he fell in love and eventually married Hannah.

Hannah had a gentle spirit about her and also had a special-needs daughter by a previous marriage. That little girl became the apple of Donnie's eye as he became the only daddy Ellie ever knew. He loved her as if she were his own child. He considered it a blessing to be her dad. His desire was that, one day, he and Hannah would have a natural-born child of their own. Fourteen years later, that dream came true when beautiful LaNita was born.

Donnie held his beautiful tiny and healthy daughter in his arms. He loved everything about her. Ellie was now fourteen years old and was very excited to have a baby sister. Photos flooded the social media with news of LaNita's arrival. Life was good; Donnie knew he was abundantly blessed, but Satan desired to have him. Little did he know the tests and trials that he would face.

Hannah and Donnie worked different shifts; he worked days, and she worked evenings and part of the night. They were able to take care of both girls and not put them into any childcare facilities. Donnie didn't mind the dirty diapers, the meals he had to prepare, and the bedtime stories he read. He enjoyed the attention he could give to his girls.

With Ellie at his side and LaNita in his arms, he started to the bedroom to put the girls to sleep. When Ellie tugged on his shirt, he turned to look at her. Wham! Bam! LaNita's head banged against the doorframe of the bedroom. She was knocked unconscious, and terror filled Donnie's heart. He was crying and praying in a panic, trying to revive this beautiful child.

"Oh god! Oh god!" he screamed to the top of his voice. He tried to breath into his baby's mouth, and then, with many attempts and no response, he—without thinking of the consequences—started to shake the four-month-old baby to help her regain consciousness. She still remained limp in his arms.

"Wake up, LaNita! God, help me, please, what can I do? She's not coming around. Yes, she is still breathing," he screamed in desperation. Ellie stood bewildered and crying beside of him. He broke into a multitude of tears as fear swept over his weak body. "I'll call Hannah, she will know what to do." Trembling, he dialed the number and tried to explain in broken sobs what had happened. In her own panic, Hannah screamed for him to call 911. She was on her way home.

Hannah arrived moments after the ambulance arrived with the police and the Child Protection Agency. Hundreds of questions filled the room. Donnie was still in a state of shock. Ellie was shaking from all of the commotion. Hannah was trying to figure everything out as the attendants transported LaNita to the ambulance and started life support. Hannah went with her baby to the hospital with sirens blazing through the neighborhood.

The police were asking all kinds of questions, "Why didn't you call 911 immediately? Did you hit the baby? Did you throw her against the wall? Did you shake her? Did you lose your temper? Do you have a habit of abusing children? How did she injure her head, did you do it? Have you ever been arrested for child abuse? Do you have a criminal record? What kind of drugs are you using? How much alcohol have you had tonight?"

Donnie was terrified as he screamed over and over, "No! No! It was an accident!"

The Child Protection Agency wanted to know if there was anyone who could take care of Ellie. Hannah's sister had been called, and Ellie left with her in distraught confusion. All of the sounds in the room faded out, and Donnie felt a strange numbness covering his body in the silence.

He was startled as he heard the police saying, "Put your hands behind your back. You're under arrest for child abuse with intention to do bodily harm." Everything became a blur, and he felt as if he would pass out. His face turned a sickening pale and grayish color; his knees knocked as his body trembled into a shake.

"You have the right to remain silent. Anything you say can and will be held against you."

"What? No? This can't be happening. I would never hurt my baby. I love her. I want to go to the hospital with her. Please, please," he begged. "You've got this all wrong!"

The policeman pushed Donnie's head down as he got into the back seat. Donnie was in shock; he couldn't even pray. He was headed to jail.

Where is God? He pondered in frozen thoughts. *This has to be a horrible nightmare.*

* * * * *

At the jail, Donnie went to booking where he was photographed and fingerprinted. He had to give up his cell phone, his money, his wallet, and personal items in his pockets and exchanged his clothes for an orange jumpsuit. He was allowed to make a phone call. He called his mother.

"Mom, Mom, I'm in a lot of trouble! I don't know how to tell you this, but I am in jail. Don't panic!" He could hear the nervousness in her voice.

"What's wrong, Donnie? Why are you in jail? What happened?"

"They think I hurt LaNita. Mom, I didn't do anything. I need some help. Oh god! I can't believe this. Mom! Mom!" His voice began to break.

Louise could feel her heart pounding faster and faster. The blood was rushing to her head, making it difficult to process the thoughts.

"Donnie, what happened to LaNita? Is she all right? I know you would never hurt her. Where is she?"

"She's at the hospital with Hannah, Mom, it looks bad, and they arrested me for child abuse. It was an accident, Mom. I'm worried about her."

"Can I come and get you out?" Louise felt the tears rolling down her cheeks. This was her son—her only child. He had always been so good. He never gave her any problems, he never uttered profanity, he had never tasted alcohol, he never used any kind of drugs, he had never even smoked a cigarette, and now, he was in jail. She couldn't believe this was happening, and she didn't know what to do! Donnie did not belong in jail. Donnie had been a late pregnancy, and she was now a disabled widow. She didn't own a car and had never learned to drive. In desperation, she felt completely helpless.

"Oh, God! Oh, God! Oh, God!" she started praying over the phone. "Help my boy, God, please, help Donnie."

"Mom." Donnie tried to comfort her. "It will be all right, you can't come and get me out." He tried to calm her down. "They haven't set my bond yet. Don't worry. Check on Hannah and LaNita for me, and Mom, I have to go. Mom, why don't you call Micki. She will know what to do. I gotta go. I love you."

He was gone; the sound of the dial tone in her ears was deafening.

After a few moments of trying to pull herself back to reality, she dialed my number. I had known her for many years and knew Donnie since his birth. They were my friends.

Louise was shaking and sobbing, and I could hear it all in her voice as she tried to talk to me.

"Micki, oh, Micki, the police put Donnie in jail. He's in jail, Micki, Donnie is in jail," she wailed.

"Calm down, Louise, try to calm down. It's hard to understand what you are saying. What about Donnie?"

"He's been arrested, he's in jail, and they said he hurt LaNita!" Her sounds became muffled with tears, and I thought she might be going into shock. She was elderly and had many physical limitations.

"What?" I shouted in disbelief. "Donnie's in jail? For hurting LaNita? No way! Try to get hold of yourself, Louise, or you are going to have a heart attack. I am coming over to check on you. Sit down and don't move. I'll be there in just a few minutes."

By the time I got there, I was shaking too. I couldn't believe this was happening, and I knew there was absolutely no way that Donnie would hurt his baby girl.

Louise lived alone in her small mobile home. When I arrived, she was sitting on her recliner with her face in her tear-filled hands. She was shaking and looked as if she was going to pass out. She was very pale, and her breathing was shallow. In panting breaths, she was finally able to tell me what she knew about the incident. I called the hospital and talked with Hannah, who also seemed to be in a state of shock. The news she had heard about the baby at that time was not good. Tests were being run. LaNita was admitted as a patient, and there was the possibility that she had bleeding in her brain because she had been shaken. Hannah was worried about the baby and also about Donnie; she was broken in spirit and feeling weak and sick. Her nerves and her world shattered.

"Please, check on Donnie for me and let me know what is going on. Call me back as soon as you can. Is he on his way to the hospital? Why on Earth would he ever shake LaNita? This is all so crazy, and I don't understand what is happening."

I spoke softly and as comforting as I could, "Hannah, he won't be at the hospital. He has been arrested and is in jail."

"Oh my god! No! No!" She was in tears again.

I tried to calm her. "I'm sure it is just the natural procedure for this type of situation. I will check on him. You just stay with LaNita, and we will keep in touch. Just know that we are praying for her and all of you."

In a panic-filled voice, she cried, "Where is Ellie? Who has Ellie?"

I explained that she was with her aunt Karen and that we would check on her too.

I hung up the phone and went over to Louise. She had always been a devoted friend. Donnie, Hannah, and the girls meant everything to her. Everything was crashing down around her. Finally, after several hours and a lot of prayer, I was able to help Louise calm down enough to drink some tea with me.

"We will get this worked out, Louise. We both know that Donnie did not intentionally hurt LaNita, and he will be all right even if he has to spend the night in jail. I will go with you tomorrow to check on him and see if he needs a lawyer or if he can get signed out on his own bond. After that is taken care of, we will go to the hospital to check on LaNita and Hannah. We just have to trust God."

With bloodshot eyes and a trembling voice, she whimpered in a very weak voice, "Where is God?"

It broke my heart to see her this way.

"He is right here with us," I spoke gently and put my arms around her. I looked directly into her face and said, "And He is right there in the jail with Donnie, and He is in the hospital with Hannah, LaNita, and the doctors. He is being a comfort to Ellie right now too. He hears our prayers, and He sees all of our tears. We just have to trust God. He is right here with us too."

"I know, I know," she said as she put her head on my shoulder to weep.

My nerves were shattered, and I felt so helpless. This was all new to me; I needed God to give me strength and direction. I knew, without a doubt, that I had to be the strong one in this situation and do everything I could to help. I stayed with Louise the rest of the night and prayed for most of the night. I know there is power and strength in prayer. I know that God can make the impossible possible. I tried very hard to keep the faith and not let doubt creep into my mind.

* * * * *

The weeks that followed were incredible. Donnie was only allowed visitors once per week with only two people visiting at a time. Hannah insisted on first visiting Donnie alone, so Louise and I waited for the second week visitation. In the meantime, I had contacted the people where Donnie worked and explained the situation. They were sympathetic and agreed to hold his position at work until things could get worked out, bond set, and Donnie released. Donnie had worked there for eighteen years. It was his first and only job. He had been a good employee and was faithful and dependable.

Donnie was placed under a hundred-thousand-dollar bond. Nobody had the ten thousand dollars he would need to get out of jail. He also needed a good attorney, and that would cost, at least, five thousand dollars more to just get started. Donnie needed to be out of jail in order to get a good attorney. Louise and I checked everywhere. I went back to Donnie's employer and asked if he could borrow money on his 401(k) retirement plan. We talked to the bondsmen, an attorney, the district attorney, the representatives at the Child Protection Agency, the arresting officers, and anyone who needed to know that we had confidence in Donnie, that he was a good person, and that the injury had definitely been an accident. We tried to get the bond reduced. We looked for anyone who might have an answer, and we continued to talk to God about the desperate situations Donnie, Hannah, LaNita, and Ellie were facing. It was a whirlwind of work and prayers. The church was praying, and many friends showed their concern.

One day, when Louise and I visited Donnie, he had been in jail for a month then, waiting for court and things to come together. He sat across from us with a glass window between. He looked thin and sickly. He was out of isolation, and we could see the other inmates walking around in the big room behind him. It was time for dinner, and Donnie asked if he could eat while he talked with us. They brought his dinner. The sickening smell of his food floated into the area where we sat. I thought about how much he liked to cook and how he enjoyed good home-cooked meals. He opened his milk and took a swallow, then he spit it out because it was soured. He had lost some weight already, but he kept his hopes and spirits high. We explained that LaNita was doing better, although she was still in the hospital. Tears filled his eyes.

"I pray every day that she will be okay. I love her so much." He stifled his words, trying to fight his emotions. "I love Ellie too. I worry about her in all of this mess." He hung his head in shame. "I've got a Bible, and they let me read it. I pray on my knees every night, and I believe I am being a witness and comfort to my cellmate. He wants me to talk about the Lord to him."

"Don't worry, Donnie, hold on to God. He is still in control."

When we left him, our emotions were strained.

* * * * *

Hannah spent most of her time at the hospital, coming home to shower and change clothes, and then, back to LaNita. Later, when we made another visit to the hospital, we were able to see LaNita, and she was improving every day. The swelling had gone down on her brain, and she had no apparent brain damage. I held the little angel in my arms and loved on her.

"Thank you, God, for answering prayers," I prayed quietly.

During the next two weeks, I carried documents from Donnie's employer to him for signatures and back to the office for processing. The sixty-mile round trip several times was worth it when Donnie was able to get a loan from his retirement fund to pay a percentage of his bond. He would be able to make monthly payments on the balance. He would still have to stand trial for the horrible charges, but he could get out of jail. However, he could not return home because of the abuse charges. He would have to find another place to live. At the time of his release, he would not be able to even visit his children. It broke his heart. He could see Hannah away from the house but was in no way allowed to go there.

Louise and I spent time with the bondsman and getting the papers in order. We paid the specified amount with the company-issued check. They would take the papers to the courthouse and jail to set everything up for Donnie's release.

The day of his release, I drove Hannah and Louise to the jail, and we waited in my car. We were not allowed to be part of the process. Our eyes were glued to the doorway where Donnie would come out. When he walked through those doors, Hannah jumped out of the car and started running toward him. He dropped his bags and started running toward her. They fell into an awesome embrace, hugging, kissing, and crying. It reminded me of a scene from a love-story movie. I could feel the dampness in my eyes. Louise was elated. When Donnie hugged her, he wiped the tears from both of their eyes. Donnie was free, at least, for the time being.

We had lunch together, and Donnie ate like he had never had any food before. It was a happy moment for all of us. We spent time together, and then, I had to take Louise and Donnie to her small mobile home. Hannah had to leave to go pick up the girls.

* * * * *

LaNita was home now and doing well. Ellie was back at home too and cried to see her daddy. It was hard for her to understand that he couldn't come home.

Since Donnie and Hannah had shared their only vehicle for transportation to and from work, it was difficult to figure out a way for both of them to use the same car. However, on Monday morning, Donnie was back on his job. He had friends volunteer to give him a ride until he could figure something else out. He stayed with Louise for a while and, then, moved in with a friend who could help him get back-and-forth to work. We managed to work out some arrangements for him and Hannah to spend time together while some friends took care of the girls. He longed to go home, to sit in his recliner, and sleep in his bed. He desperately longed to be with his family. Those unbearable, lonely nights were filled with grief and tears.

* * * * *

I took him to visit with a lawyer who said he would accept his case. He was a tough attorney and would allow Donnie to make payments to him, but he needed one thousand dollars up front before he would start.

A thousand more dollars? Where in the world could that money come from? We wondered.

I wrestled with my thoughts all though the night, praying and seeking God for answers. It was near the dawning of the day when I felt the peace of God as if I heard him say, "Ask, and it shall be given." I remembered the scriptures as it burned in my mind. I knew what I had to do and finally closed my eyes in peaceful sleep.

When I awoke, I went to my computer and started typing a form. God inspired me to write a statement in testimony as to Donnie's character, with signatures from people who knew him, who could not believe that he was guilty of intentional child abuse. We knew him as a loving husband to his wife and wonderful father to his children. A Christian who served God and the Church. A kind and gentle person and a good neighbor. I referenced the scripture, "Blessed are the merciful for they shall obtain mercy." I also asked for financial support to help raise one thousand dollars for his attorney. I typed lines for signatures and telephone numbers in the event anyone would need to call them for verification. Each page allowed space for approximately twenty signatures and phone numbers. I made many copies to be distributed at a couple of different churches and for family, friends, and neighbors who were concerned about the situation. Donnie, Hannah, and I began to deliver them. The response was amazing. We ended up with one hundred signatures and one thousand dollars. We took the signed papers to his attorney, along with the thousand dollars. We also presented a copy to the district attorney and the Child Protection Agency.

Amazingly, his story never reached the media. God is a good God.

In the weeks that followed before the trial, Donnie was allowed supervised visitation with his children and, eventually, at their home. He still was not allowed to stay there with them.

Finally, after a long process, the trail was in session. The charges for intentional child abuse with intent to do bodily harm was reduced to neglect. The courts believed it was an accident. Donnie was placed on probation; he still had to work hard and make payments to the lawyer and repay his 401(k) loan, but he was free. Free to go home, free to spend time with his children, free to get back to some sense of normal living. Donnie was free, indeed! He was so grateful to all of us who helped him and to God above for making a way where there seemed to be no way.

They are still my friends and close as family to me. Donnie loves me like his second mother, and he calls my husband his adoptive dad. My prayer is that God will continue to bless them and use them for His glory.

This chapter closes with gratitude to my Creator for using me in distressed situations. I know new assignments await me as a volunteer in service for the King of kings and my Creator. I am reminded of the story of Esther in the Bible and, somehow, know that we were born to serve for such a time as this.

Even through our darkest hours, we can still feel the working presence of our powerful God.

7

Her Name Was Elizabeth

I had no idea what Elizabeth had been through in her past, when my mom recommended her as a live-in babysitter for me. The only thing my mom really knew about her was that she seemed to be a sweet girl who had recently moved into their neighborhood. When Elizabeth had taken walks down the dirt road behind their house, Mom had chatted with her over the fence. I desperately needed someone soon, so I interviewed her quickly. She seemed sweet enough and eagerly responded with a big yes. She was twenty-four years old, and her family had no objection to her decision. Her dad was deceased, and she and her mother had been living in a crowded situation at her brother's home. She was more than happy to have her own room in my house, and she instantly fell in love with my two young sons. Bruce was six, and Ricky was only four years old. My office was less than five minutes away from my house, so I felt secure with the situation. The school was close by, so Elizabeth and Ricky would walk Bruce to school every morning and, then, be there at closing to walk him home. It was a blessing to me just to have the extra help. We, soon, discovered there was a little problem going on.

At night, every night, Elizabeth would scream in her sleep; she would cry, sobbing tears, and that sound sent both boys running to my bed. My husband was away at school in Florida, so most nights, I was sleeping between both my boys.

Finally, after several weeks of sleepless nights, I got out of bed and slowly opened the door to Elizabeth's room. She was tossing and turning violently, sobbing, moaning, and seemingly terrorized by some horrible nightmare. As I watched her for a few minutes, I knew she needed help. I went to her bedside and gently began to wake her up.

"Elizabeth, Elizabeth, wake up, you are having a bad dream."

"Elizabeth, honey, it is only a dream. Can you hear me?"

She awoke from her terror and sat straight up in the bed. She was throwing her arms wildly, and her face was as pale as a ghost. She was trembling so bad that the entire bed was shaking. When she finally regained some composure, she looked at me with wide eyes.

"What's wrong? Are the boys okay? Why are you out of bed?" Her questions came in breathless concern.

"No, honey, you were having a terrible nightmare. I just got up to check on you. Do you feel like getting up for a little while? It's almost morning. The coffee smells good. Let's share a cup while you get calmed down."

She walked into the kitchen in her robe. She was heavyset, about 260 pounds, with short straight hair. You could tell by her demeanor that life had been hard or cruel for her, but her heart was happy, just like a young girl who didn't want to face the reality of growing up.

"Be careful. That coffee is very hot." I smiled as I handed her the cup.

Her face was looking down to the floor, and she apparently didn't want to look me in the eyes.

"What's wrong, honey, do you remember your dream? Are you still upset?"

She responded with a quick no and a very nervous look on her face.

"Well, do you want to talk about it? Can I help you?"

There was another quick no, but I really wanted to get to the bottom of the situation.

"It's okay to talk about it, Elizabeth. When were you raped?"

Immediately, her face was filled with horror, her eyes welled with tears, and she began to shake.

"Who told you? Who told you? How did you know?" she bellowed out at me.

"Calm down. It's all right. You can trust me. Have you ever told anyone before?"

She broke down and began to spill out her story of sorrows in great detail to me, and my heart was breaking as she shared her life with me. She had never breathed a word of her story to another person.

It started after her daddy died when she was five years old. Her dad had been so proud of her and loved her so very much. She was his little angel. Her mother, Lucille, on the other hand, had not wanted the pregnancy or the daughter that was born of her. She expressed to the child many times that she wished her daddy had let her do the abortion. Over and over, she screamed at Elizabeth, telling her that her life was ruined the day she was born. She never loved or cared for Elizabeth, and she didn't mind who knew it. When her daddy died suddenly, Elizabeth was left to be cared for by her cruel mother. Carl, Lucille's 18-year-old son, immediately joined the army.

It wasn't even a year before Lucille had everyone calling her Lucy as she made the scene at the local dance halls. That is where she met and fell in love with Sam. Elizabeth didn't like Sam from the beginning. He was always smiling with a wicked grin, and Elizabeth didn't like the way he looked at her. He tried to make up for the way her mother treated her, but it made Elizabeth uncomfortable. She would run to her mother for comfort which never really came. Lucy wanted Elizabeth to like Sam, hoping he would ask her to marry him. They seemed to have a lot of fun together, but Elizabeth knew he would never be her daddy.

When Elizabeth was seven years old, Lucy and Sam were married, and they all moved to a big house in the country. She did not like the new school, and the big house was creepy and dark. They were far away from her daddy's sisters, whom Lucy missed, and any cousins that she used to play with when her daddy was alive. Elizabeth grew lonely and scared. Lucy and Sam would stay up late at night, drinking beer and laughing. It was weird for Elizabeth to see how they behaved, kissing and teasing each other in front of her. It disturbed Elizabeth to see Sam putting his hands all over her mother.

When Elizabeth was eight years old, things got worse. Lucy had a chance to go on vacation with some of the girls at her work. They would be gone for a whole week. At first, Sam was upset with the idea, but then, he figured it would be all right. Elizabeth wanted to know what would happen to her; could she stay with her aunts? Could she go with her mom?

The answer was an emphatic. "No, Sam's going to take care of you. It's just for a little while, and I will be back before you know it."

As Lucy waved bye, tears flowed down Elizabeth's cheeks. She really didn't know if she would ever see her mother again. What if she didn't come back? These thoughts filled her head as Sam tried to comfort her. He laid his big hands on her tiny back, rubbing them around in little circles, and told her that everything would be just fine. Elizabeth broke free from him and ran to her hiding place up on the hill as she heard him curse and say, "Just be that way." Then, he went into the house and began to guzzle his beer. Elizabeth stayed on the hill until almost dark. It was late summer, so around nine o'clock, a bright full moon crested the sky, and the night sky was filled with what seemed like a million stars. She walked slowly down the hill and peeked through the open screen door. She could see Sam passed out on the couch, snoring loudly. She went inside and crept up the stairs to her room and crawled into her bed. She felt safe, at least, for that night.

The next morning, she was up early and fixed a bowl of cereal to eat. Sam was still sprawled out on the couch. The screen door slammed behind her as she scurried up the hill. It woke Sam up. In a stupor of a hangover, he was on the porch, yelling for her to get back to the house. She hid behind some bushes and watched as Sam finally gave up and went back inside. She was scared. Sam had never really been mean to her, but she knew he was a different person when he drank too much. That's when Lucille and Sam had the most fights.

Later that afternoon, she saw Sam in the backyard, a wooded area, and she quietly crept in through the front door. She fixed a peanut-butter-and-jelly sandwich because she was hungry and drank a glass of milk. The jug of milk was heavy, and she spilled some on the table, just as she heard Sam coming into the house. He was sober and smiling. He was being nice to her and not scolding her for spilling the milk. He told her she was a big girl now—the woman of the house—and that he intended to treat her nice. All of that made Elizabeth feel better and a little safer. Maybe Sam wasn't so bad after all. He wasn't even drinking when he tucked her into bed that night, and he told her a funny bedtime story. She was very tired and went to sleep as soon as he turned off the light.

The sound of a loud crash downstairs woke her out of a peaceful sleep. Sam was stumbling around and had knocked something off the table. He was cursing, and Elizabeth knew he was drunk again. She pulled the covers up over her head but couldn't go back to sleep. After a while, everything was quiet, and she dozed off to sleep again.

She felt cold and reached sleepily for her covers but couldn't find them. She opened her eyes and saw Sam standing beside her bed. He was holding her covers, and he was naked. Her heart froze with fear as he motioned for her to be very quiet, then he crawled in bed with her and pulled her small body against his. She panicked and tried to push him away, she scratched at him, she cried bitterly. He slapped her, and he hurt her—he hurt her really bad. After he raped her, he told her that if she ever told anybody what had happened, he would kill her and kill her mother too. He reached over to the bedside table and picked up a gun and held it against her face. He meant it; he would kill both of them.

That horrible week alone with Sam, the same thing happened, night after night. Elizabeth was in such shock and distress that she couldn't get out of bed during the day. Fear gripped her tiny body, and she thrashed, screamed, and clawed at Sam, but he just laughed with a wicked, evil sound. The day before her mom was to return, he made her get up, take a bath, change her clothes, and reminded her she could never say a word about it to anyone. She believed he would kill her and her mom. She believed it so strongly that she had never told anyone until she was telling me that night. After Lucille came home, Sam never touched Elizabeth again.

When late August rolled around, Elizabeth was thrilled at the idea of going back to school and being in a room full of girls and boys her age. However, since Sam wasn't sure she would really keep her mouth shut, he kept her out of school. He told Lucille that she couldn't go to school; she just wasn't a normal little girl. Sam convinced Lucille that something was dreadfully wrong with her. Lucille said that was nothing new to her; she agreed that Elizabeth wasn't bright and never wanted to be a part of her life.

Elizabeth had actually become a trembling wreck. Sam arranged for her to see one of his doctor friends. The doctor could see she was traumatized and believed she had been that way for a long time. Elizabeth was in third grade when the doctor signed the papers that she was incompetent. Arrangements were made to get her a check for her disabilities, and she was locked in her room most of the time.

On one occasion, her aunts made the visit to see about her, but by now, Elizabeth looked the part of a dangerous child. She was locked in her room when they arrived. It had been a few years since they had seen her. Lucille and Sam explained that she just had not been able to cope with the loss of her father, and there was nothing they could do to help her. When the aunts wanted to see her, they cautioned them about her behavior and said she was not allowed to have access to anything glass or any knives or things like that. Their first glimpse of Elizabeth was sad. She had gained a lot of weight, her hair was cropped off above her ears, and she wouldn't even look them in the eyes. She was wearing a dress that was way too big, wrinkled, and dirty. Finally, after they talked to her quietly, she seemed to recognize them and ran to them, sobbing. As Sam and Lucille entered the room, Elizabeth broke free and cowered in the corner. Both her aunts left, feeling overwhelmed at what they thought had happened to Elizabeth. They lost touch except for an occasional birthday card for Elizabeth or a follow-up phone call to Lucille.

Lucille and Sam spent the disability income on alcohol and drugs, and none of it was used for Elizabeth. This went on for years, and when Elizabeth was nineteen years old, Sam died from alcohol poisoning and took his secret to the grave and hell with him. Lucille moved to North Carolina to live with relatives, and Elizabeth was admitted to a mental institution where she began the long process of recovery.

At the mental institution, Elizabeth began to heal in her mind. Her aunts paid regular visits and regained the love of Elizabeth. She worked on crafts and began to relax around other people. She was still very nervous and found it difficult to look anybody in the eyes. Eventually, she was released and came back to live with Lucille who, once again, had control of the disability check. She had changed and softened a little since she had gotten older, although she still warned people that Elizabeth was dangerous—no knives, no glass items— and she still didn't care what happened to her child.

That's when Elizabeth used to take walks by my mom's house. Mom invited her to church, and she attended regularly. She made friends, and her life had improved to almost normal, except for the nightmares which always came when she closed her eyes in sleep.

By the time she finished telling me her story, we were both in tears. My heart was crushed for her.

"You never told anybody what happened?" I looked at her with questioning eyes.

"Never told anybody, not until tonight." She sobbed but seemed somewhat relieved that she had finally got it out into the open.

"Well, Elizabeth," I comforted her, "tonight is the night that it is all finally over. You will never have to live with that secret again."

"You won't tell Lucille, will you? I don't want anything to do with her."

"Not if you don't want me to." I sighed. "But I am going to help you."

"How? What can you do about it?"

"Well, for one thing, Elizabeth has a horrible past that needs to be put behind her. You know you have two names in the name Elizabeth, and I will never call you Elizabeth again. So what do you prefer—Liz or Beth?"

She smiled at me and said, "I like Beth."

"Okay, then, from now on, you are Beth, and Elizabeth is gone. Beth has never had these horrible things happen to her. Beth is the girl that goes to church, that loves God, that wants to make something better out of her life. Now, is that you?"

"It sure is!" She smiled and hugged me very tightly. "Thank you."

I never called her Elizabeth again. Beth and I became the closest of friends, and she continued to live with me for years. During that time, she made her first visit to a beauty parlor, learned how to wear her makeup, lost over one hundred pounds, and had her first store-bought dress. She could finally look everyone in the eyes; she wasn't afraid or nervous every time a man walked into the room. She was finally happy and grew into maturity. She loved God and was a willing worker in the church. She eventually had her first date and her own apartment. She met and married a very handsome man and gave birth to her own baby boy.

We are still close friends, almost like sisters, to this day. She is a very special person and one of the biggest challenges ever given to me as the Creator's temporary.

* * * * *

Sometimes, my assignments are short, and sometimes, like the one with Beth, they become very long, but they are worth every precious moment when God puts me into someone's life or even in someone's way. The glory belongs to Him, and the blessings are mine.

I have had people ask me on numerous occasions why I don't just settle down somewhere. Actually, the truth is that since I left my parents' home at the age of nineteen, I have been on the move. God takes me from one place and one situation to another. This world is not my home because I am not at home yet. I am a citizen of heaven, and it is all in a life's work. Where He leads me, I will follow; I am on assignment.

Being kind to the hopeless can change their lives and yours.

8

Brave and Bold

Larry was handsome, owned his own business, wealthy, and definitely a ladies' man, but he was also an alcoholic. He loved the nightlife, big parties, and enjoyed life to the fullest. When I took a job with him, I was paid a two-dollar per hour raise over my last salary. I just had a feeling that this would be a perfect place to work. I was in a one-girl office, and the workload wasn't heavy at all. The office was spacious, and the television stayed on all day. Customers would come and go, and I enjoyed meeting all of them. The specialty printing shop was in a larger building attached to the office. Everyone there seemed to enjoy their jobs.

Before he even saw my resume, Larry learned from friends and references that I was a Christian. I appreciated the respect he showed to me, and I liked him as a person. Many times, he would pull up a chair across from my desk, and I could tell he had been hitting the bottle. He was still respectful, but he took pleasure in sharing all of his troubles and life problems with me. He could talk for hours about his past marriage, the way his ex-wife had treated him; he expounded on the way his love life was going with his new girlfriends and that he wished he could find the right woman. He would laugh and had a lot of humor in his tales of woe and was pretty entertaining with some of his stories. He really had nothing better to do, and I was a good listener, even though it did interfere with my work sometimes. I always managed to lend a listening ear and tried to give him good advice. I told him that if he would consider changing his life and live for God, then God would direct his path and lead him to the right person and happiness again.

I witnessed to his son who also worked in the shop and many of the other employees.

I was so surprised when, one day, while Larry was out of the office, his son, Jim, brought a friend into the office to talk about an order. They both walked in without saying a word to me, as they were in deep conversation. Jim's buddy apparently was not used to being cautious around women, and in his conversation with Jim, he began to use some nasty language. I looked up from my desk just in time to see Jim waving his arms in the air, anxiously trying to stop his friend from using the vile language. His friend was startled and looked at him questioningly.

"What? What's going on, Jim?"

"Hold it down, Buddy. You can't talk like that in here," Jim spoke just above a whisper.

"What's happened? Why?" He blinked with a weird expression.

Holding his hand in front of him, Jim pointed his thumb toward me in a quiet motion. "God is over there!"

"Ohhh," Buddy said quietly, as if the office had become a church. He shook his head in a hushed okay, signaling that he understood.

Jim motioned for them to head to the door, and they quietly left the office.

I couldn't believe what had just happened. I was shocked and amazed at the same time. What an honor it was to be respected in such a manner that they both could sense the presence of God in that room through my life. I smiled to myself and thanked God for my testimony. I still get a chuckle out of it today when I remember the way they looked and acted. If only more people would respect God and His presence in that way, the world would be a better place.

Time passed, and I enjoyed my work there. Once, when the workload was extra heavy, Larry called in a temp to help me out. When she arrived the first day, we got along fine, but I knew there was a certain smell about her that indicated she was using vodka to help her make it through the day. She was attractive and pleasant, but she kept her little bottle in her purse, and I had seen her hitting it a few times. Larry was out of town that first day, but when he came back to work, they hit if off just fine. He would take her to his big office, and they would chat for hours. After the first week, Larry burst through the door to my office just as Jim came in from the shop. Larry was so frazzled. He yelled to Jim and me, "Hey, she's passed out in my office on the bearskin rug. What will I do?"

I ran into his office while Jim tried to calm his dad down.

"No, you're going to stay out here, Dad. Micki will see what's going on!"

"But I have got to go back in there," he whined.

"No way, Dad! You just have to get calmed down. Sit down."

Larry was pretty drunk too, and he slumped down on the couch in my office.

I went in to check on the woman as she was struggling to get to her feet.

"I don't feel so good." She tried to straighten out her clothes. I was glad she still had them on. I talked to her for a while and asked if she needed a ride home. She said she would call her daughter to pick her up. When her daughter arrived, I let her out by the back door in Larry's office. When I came back to my office, Larry was sound asleep on the couch in my office. I was thankful that it was almost five o'clock and went ahead and locked up the office and turned on the closed sign. We never saw the temp again. That's the way it was working there; you just never knew what to expect next.

A few weeks later, Larry was sitting at my desk again, spilling his stories to me. This time, he started to get into religion.

"I know where I am going when I die," he spoke in a staggered, drunken, slurry tone.

I raised my eyebrows and looked at him. "Do you, Larry? Do you really know where you will go when you die?"

"Yeah," he drawled it out. "I'm going up." And he raised his hands toward the sky.

I thought to myself, *How can you be so deceived? How do you plan to get there living the way you do? God, help me to keep my self-control.* I prayed under my breath, but it was too late.

I felt a holy boldness start in my feet, and it pushed me to a standing position, with both hands spread out on my desk, with a firm and serious look in my eyes, and I moved close to his face.

"Larry, you are going to split hell wide open if you die in the shape you are in! You have to change your way of living and get things right with God Almighty if you want to make heaven your home!" I sat back down in my chair, shaking a little and thinking that I had probably just lost my job.

"What do you mean, Micki?" He looked bewildered. "Do you think I am a bad person?"

"No, Larry." I softened. "You are not a bad person. You just need to ask Jesus to forgive you for your sins and start on a new life. Jesus is the life, and He is the only way for you to go up."

He rocked back in his chair and stared at me.

"Oh, I am not ready for that—not yet." He smiled. "Not yet. Maybe someday."

I continued to tell him that God loved him and wanted to help him. He was listening, and I spoke softly.

"Larry, would you promise me one thing? If you are ever in a car wreck or come face-to-face with death, would you please, at least, ask Jesus to forgive you if you have time? Would you pray and ask Him to save you? Would you promise me that?"

He had suddenly grown very sober as he replied, "I will, I promise."

Two weeks passed, and all of us were getting ready for the big Christmas barbeque. The guys on the back had a big cooker ready, and we were all bringing special dishes to add to the celebration. We would be out of work for a few days for the Christmas holiday.

I was still at home, just finishing up my special dish and wrapping it to take to work, when the radio announced that there had been a fatal accident on one of the county roads. There were always a lot of accidents when there was sleet and ice on the roads, so I didn't pay it much attention and turned off the radio before I heard more details.

When I walked in my office, I knew something was terribly wrong. Jim and the crew were there; they had just heard the news. Larry had been killed in an accident. Our hearts were broken. It was only two days till Christmas. He had come in early that morning, sober and happy about the special Christmas party. Apparently, he had forgotten something that he was going to bring to the party and headed back to his condo to pick it up. I don't know if he was speeding, but when he hit black ice on the county road, he lost control of the vehicle, and the car sailed through the air for approximately fifty feet and crashed into some huge boulders beside the road. Mostly likely, he died on impact. I wondered, *Did you realize what was happening, Larry? Did you find time to pray? Did you remember your promise?*

The funeral services were beautiful, and he was greatly loved and honored by his family and friends. Jim took over the family business, and I continued to work for him, but things were not the same without Larry.

Once, Jim came into my office and sat down on the chair across from me. As we talked about how Larry used to do that, Jim spoke quietly.

"Well, at least, he's in heaven now. He's better off."

I felt a twinge in my heart as I said, "I hope so, Jim, and someday, we can all see him again."

Sometimes, God puts us in places for a season and for many different reasons. When the Holy Spirit moves on you to say something, it could be words of encouragement, wisdom, or even a warning. We just need to be willing to speak to others at the time God tells us to. None of us knows what the future holds, but we can be sure that God holds the future.

Eventually, you may be faced in your assignments with difficult situations when you know that what you say may affect your job and even your life. Say it anyway. We are on assignment in the service of the true King. We must help to build His kingdom by being obedient to His commands.

Fear is diminished when you speak the words that God burns in your heart.

9

The Happiness Miracle

Roy was a sad little boy, about seven years old, when I first met him. He lived with his dad, Jake, his stepmother, Hazel, and four stepbrothers and two stepsisters. He never really knew his mom, Gloria. Gloria had left him with Jake when she disappeared with her newfound love and moved from the east coast to the west coast. Jake played with a band and was on the road most of the time; that left Roy with Hazel and her six children. Roy was the outcast.

During church visitation, we happened to go to their house to invite them to church. I was surprised to see Jake. I had known him in my early teens. He was between gigs and was in town at that time, so he invited us in. My friend, Lisa, was visiting the neighborhood with me. We were introduced to Jake's family. Hazel was an attractive woman, but the signs of a rough life made her look old and tired. She had the four boys by a previous marriage, but the two younger girls belonged to her and Jake. When no one bothered to introduce us to Roy, I introduced myself and held out my hand to him.

"What's your name, young man?" I smiled as he shook my hand, and he replied, "My name is Roy. Jake's my daddy."

He was interrupted by two of his annoying brothers.

"Yeah, he thinks he is Roy Rogers! But he ain't."

The older boy chimed in, "That's right, and he don't have no mama either!"

Hazel spoke roughly, "Now, boys, you shouldn't talk like that in front of our visitors. Why don't both of you just go back to your room and play your games and let us do the talking."

The boys slouched off as Roy just sat quietly on the floor. We invited them to our church and told them about the great classes we had for teens and children.

The two other boys started grinning at each other and left for another room. They talked loud enough for me to hear them.

"We ain't never been to church, and we don't want to go either."

"Church is for sissies, and we wouldn't like it anyway."

I glanced over at Jake. "You have never taken your kids to church?" I questioned. "I remember when you used to go every Sunday as a teen."

Jake shrugged. "Well, you know how it is. My busiest times are the weekends with the band, and that don't leave much time for going to church. A man's gotta make a living. Hazel could take them if she would." He scowled up his face as he turned and pointed a finger toward her.

Hazel's face turned a bright-red. "Don't you go blaming me. Getting these kids up to get to school every day of the week is hard enough on me. Sunday is my day of rest!"

It looked like our visit might be getting too long, so we got up from the couch and started to say our goodbyes.

The two girls had been busy reading some books without paying us much attention at all.

We turned to leave when a small quiet voice said, "I'd like to go to church."

It was Roy.

Hazel looked at him and, with an unkind tone, said, "Well, well, well, if you would go to church, I'd be happy to get up and take you. At least, I wouldn't have to put up with you for a couple of hours on Sunday morning."

I bent down to eye level and looked into Roy's big brown eyes. "I would love to see you in church, Roy. Aren't you about seven years old? I believe you would be in my Sunday-school class."

"Can I go, Dad?" He was excited.

"Looks like you can, Roy. If I am in town, I'll take you and drop you off, then I have to get to my gig or practice. Hazel will pick you up, ain't that right, Hazel?"

"Humph" was all she could say.

"We will be looking for you, Roy, and praying for you too. See you Sunday."

"Thanks." He quietly closed the door behind us.

Before we could get to our car, we could hear the quarreling going on inside the house.

* * * * *

It was early on Sunday morning, and I was running copies for some classes. I noticed Jake pulled up in the parking lot and a small, little boy jumped out of the car and ran to the church entrance. I left the copier and went to meet Roy. It was still forty-five minutes before the services started, and the sanctuary was still empty. I didn't want him to be alone.

"Good morning, Roy." I smiled and attempted to give him a hug, but he seemed a little reluctant when he looked around at the emptiness.

"Where's everybody at?" He looked puzzled. "Are we the only ones here today?"

"Oh, no! You are just early. This place will be filled with happy faces very soon. You will hear some wonderful music and hear some great singing."

"Whew!" He tried to smile. "I was about to think you was just going to preach to me."

I couldn't help but grin. "No, others will be here, and I'm not even the preacher."

"You're not?" He looked puzzled.

"Come on with me. You can help me run some copies, and I could use a little help. The preacher will be here soon. You'll see."

We ran the copies, and then, beautiful organ music began to flow through the air. I showed Roy where his Sunday-school class would be, and then, we returned to the sanctuary. Roy's big brown eyes were full of surprise when he saw the people greeting each other and then finding their seats. We sat down on the front pew. He was fascinated with the music and the singing. When it was time to go to their classes, a young boy named Timmy introduced himself and volunteered to show Roy to his class. Off they went together into a whole new world of learning for Roy. I have to admit he was faithful in getting Jake to drop him off at church every Sunday morning, but he wanted more. He asked if kids could come to the Sunday-night services.

"Of course, children are always welcome in our church. Do you think Hazel or Jake would bring you?"

"Don't know, but I can try to get them to."

Well, Jake brought him about three times, and Hazel managed to drop Roy off twice.

* * * * *

It was cold outside and raining on one particular Sunday night when Roy came in. He was drenched from the rain. He was wearing a light jacket and had nothing to cover his head. He took off his jacket and, still shivering, sat down on the front pew. The church was warm and so was the spirit among the people. He soon forgot about his problems and warmed up.

After church, I had to go to the back for a short meeting with some of the ladies. I told Roy to stay right there and look for his mom or dad to pick him up.

"She's not my mom." The expression on his face was very sad. "Dad has a gig tonight, out of town. She might not come to get me."

"Oh, I am sure she will, Roy."

"I don't know. She said if I liked church so much, I could just live here." He grimaced.

"Now, Roy, she was probably just kidding with you. Watch for her out the window. I have to meet with the ladies." I tousled his auburn-colored hair and told him goodbye, then I left the sanctuary.

I thought to myself, *He is such a sweet boy but so lonely. How can his parents treat him that way?* I mused, *It is like they really don't care for him at all. He had mentioned to me many times of the way he was mistreated by all of them. He said he felt like he didn't belong there. He was not abused physically, except by his brothers, but he was only a little boy who was already broken. But God, what could I do?* The thoughts kept racing through my mind. I continued in prayer for Roy and went to my meeting.

The meeting held longer than I had hoped. When I went back to the sanctuary to pick up my coat, I was startled to see Roy sitting on the pew, crying.

"She didn't come," he whimpered. "I looked at every car, and she didn't come after me."

I pulled him into my arms to soothe his hurt. "Don't worry, I will take you home."

It was about 10:30 p.m. when I pulled into their drive. The rain was still coming down heavy, and it was very cold. I walked him to the door and knocked. No one came to the door. I knocked again and turned the knob to open the door, but it was locked. Roy and I beat on the door for a few minutes before someone yelled, "I'm coming, hold your horses."

Roy's oldest stepbrother, Buddy, opened the door. "Huh? I guess you did find a way home. Why'd you come back? We don't want you here."

"You can stop that kind of talk right now!" I interrupted him. "Where's Hazel?"

"Aww, she's asleep." He yawned. "And I'm not about to wake her up."

"Just tell her that I want to have a talk with her and Jake when he gets back in town."

I turned to Roy. "Now get out of those wet clothes and go to bed. Tomorrow's a school day. I will see you again soon." I turned to Buddy. "You need to get back to bed too, and you better leave Roy alone." I stepped back out into the rain. My face was hot, and my eyes were already wet.

I sat in my car and talked to God quietly, "God, you have put me in a lot of places, but this situation is impossible. If this is a divine assignment, I am helpless." Just then, I clearly heard words reminding me, "With God, all things are possible!"

God's plans are not always the same as our plans; His ways are not our ways; but His ways are so much more wonderful than anything we could even dream of.

* * * * *

I hadn't heard from my old friend, Fran Dire, in a very long time, but she was a sweet and wonderful memory in my mind on many occasions. Sometimes, when I would think about the times we had pastored the little church out in the country in South Carolina, I could see the loving faces of all of the people. One face that especially stood out was Fran and her husband, Milton. They were a precious couple. They loved us and loved our children. She was always available when I needed someone to watch my kids or to do emergency babysitting. Many times, she and Milton would just want to take them to spend the weekend at their home. They had been married for years and never had any children. I remember sitting at her kitchen table with enough food prepared to feed a small army. We always enjoyed their friendship and fellowship. My two boys loved her dearly, and we did too. They were heartbroken when we had the call from the Lord to move on to another town. With tear-filled eyes, we said our goodbyes.

"It's hard enough to lose the two of you." She wept. "But you're taking our boys too."

"They are the only two kids that ever really seemed like ours."

After all of the hugs, kisses, promises, and tears, we said goodbye to our dear friends.

When I had a problem or needed to talk to somebody, I would call her, and she would do the same. For several years, it was a weekly thing, then monthly as time went on, and things hindered our time to just chat with each other.

I woke up from my reminiscing and immediately thought, *I have to call Fran.*

It was wonderful to hear her cheery voice on the phone. We talked about so many things. When she asked me how things were going in my life, I told her about the problems with Roy and what he was going through. She couldn't believe what was happening to him.

"That is a horrible situation!" she countered. "Just send him to me, I'll take care of him."

"What? Are you kidding me? Would you let him come and visit with you and Milt?"

She resounded with, "You know us, and we would love to have a boy around. It is almost Christmas—only three weeks away. If you talk to his folks, we would love to celebrate Christmas holidays with him, and he could go back before school starts in January."

"Wow," I exclaimed. "That would be an amazing Christmas gift for Roy."

"It would be for us too. We would make sure his Christmas was merry and bright. Do you think they would let him come?"

"I can't be sure, but I am certainly going to ask them."

Fran was already getting excited when she said, "Let me know as soon as possible. I will have to get started on things! I just can't wait to tell Milt."

* * * * *

I had my visit with Jake and Hazel, and it went very well. I wanted to talk with them before I ever mentioned it to Roy.

Jake's response was "I don't see why not, if he wants to go. We don't care. It would probably be good for him."

Hazel chimed in with "It would be good for us too—one less mouth to feed. Are they going to buy his Christmas stuff too?"

I told them that Roy wouldn't have to worry about a thing, and that was that.

I talked to Roy, and he was overjoyed. I told him how kind and sweet Fran and Milt were and how he would love being out in the country for the holidays. I told him about Rex, their big fuzzy dog that he could play with and that he was sure to have lots of food and treats in their home. The day school was out for the holidays. He was packed to leave.

He waved bye to Jake and Hazel while the other kids looked out the windows. Roy never looked back. We made the one-hundred-mile trip to South Carolina, and it was love at first sight between the three of them—well four of them, counting Rex.

Even before Christmas day, Roy had lots of new clothes, boots, jackets, and more. Christmas was very exciting in their home. Roy had gifts under the Christmas tree like he had never had before. He never received a call from Jake or Hazel, not even on Christmas day, but it didn't bother him at all.

Too soon, it was almost time for them to bring Roy back home. Fran called me, obviously upset.

"Roy doesn't want to go back home, and we don't want him to either."

"We are praying to God that they will let us keep him, at least, for now. If they will give us permission, we will enroll him in a school down here. It is only five months until school is out for the summer. "I promise, if he wants to go back home then or if they demand it, we will bring him there. Can you talk to them again or have them call us? He will just be visiting, and there's nothing illegal about that."

"Fran, I will do what I can, but we all really need to talk to God and to Jake about all of this."

When I approached Jake and Hazel, they told me it couldn't have happened at a better time. Jake had gotten the call from California about playing in the band out there, and they were already packing things up, getting ready to move. In my heart, I wondered if they just planned to move on without telling or taking Roy, but I didn't ask. I didn't want to know.

Jake and Hazel and the kids moved to California, and Roy made his home with Fran and Milton. It wasn't very long before he was calling them Mom and Dad. After six years, when Roy became a teenager, Fran and Milton were able to legally adopt Roy. He lived there; they loved each other. Roy had a home and a mom and a dad who loved him, and Fran and Milt finally had their own son.

Roy finished school, and as a young man, he joined the air force. He fell in love with a lovely girl; they had several children. Fran and Milton were now grandparents. Roy and his wife made their home in Mississippi where she was born, but they made many visits to South Carolina and spent holidays together with Grandma Fran and Poppy Milt.

The last I heard of Jake and Hazel, they had split up. Their children were grown and soon scattered all over the United States. Jake died before Roy ever saw him again, but Roy located his two half sisters and visited them and met their husbands and his nieces and nephews.

This is a true and amazing story of the things that God can do. Only His precious guiding—His precious timing—could intertwine the lives and dreams of this family the way God did.

Yes, I was used in this assignment, but it wasn't me that worked it out—only God.

He touched the lives and hearts and minds of Jake and Hazel, Fran and Milton, and a boy named Roy who wanted to go to church.

Remember, God is always in control. After all, is there anything that God can't do?

10

Monster or Miracle

The first time I drove by Marci's house, I was shocked. It wasn't even Halloween, but the iron fence around her yard was decorated with small skulls, demons, devils, and wicked paraphilia. The weeds were growing tall, and the scene was spooky, to say the least. I drove slowly and wondered what kind of people lived there. Chill bumps prickled my skin, and I could feel evil spirits brooding somewhere out there. It was definitely the kind of place I needed to stay away from, but I had a feeling that God had a brand-new assignment for me. I whispered under my breath, "I'd rather not, Lord. Not this time." He wasn't paying any attention to me.

"It gives me the creeps." He still wasn't listening to me.

I took a deep breath and drove on.

* * * * *

My son, now married, lived in the country, and to visit with him, I had to drive by that house.

During one of my visits, I asked my daughter-in-law, Katie, about the house down the hill.

"Oh, you mean the scary one?" She laughed. "Don't worry, that's where Marci lives."

"Do you know her?"

"Well, we have spoken to each other a couple of times. She lives by herself with only her six little dogs for company. I was taking a walk down the dirt road one morning, and she was outside. You know me, Mom, I always have to say hello."

"Really?" I quizzed her, "What kind of person is she? Did she forget to take her decorations down from last Halloween?"

"Oh, you can ask Chris about it. I didn't say anything to her about those things."

"What do you mean ask Chris? Surely, my grandson hasn't been down there."

Katie tried to change the subject.

"I really need to get dinner started. Bruce will be home soon, and I know he will be hungry. I have to feed my man, you know. Do you want to help?" Katie moved toward the kitchen.

"Sure, I'd love to help, but you didn't answer my question. What's going on with Chris?"

"Now, Mom, you aren't going to like this, but Chris is twenty-four years old, and he needs to get a job. He just wants to hang out here at the house, playing video games, or take off somewhere with his friends, and we are tired of it."

"So isn't he trying to make any efforts? After all, he is a smart young man."

Katie sighed. "Well, it has come to this, Mom. Bruce and I told him if he didn't get a job, he would have to move out. He really got angry and slammed the door and walked away. He said he would find his own place to live where he could be his own man."

"When did this happen? Where is he?" I gasped.

"Actually, it has been about three weeks now, and he found a place right away. He's getting free room and board and making a little money so he can buy gas and keep his car going."

"Where is he?" I worried as most grandmothers do. "Have you seen him and talked to him?"

"Don't worry about it." Katie rattled some pots and pans. "We all made up, and he is helping this older woman run her errands. She doesn't drive her truck and needed someone to take her places like the grocery store, the doctor, and wherever she wanted to go. He is all right!"

I placed the dinner plates on the table and started to pour the tea.

"Katie, you know as well as I do, this is an evil world we live in, and sometimes, older women just want to take advantage of young men."

"No worries." Katie laughed. "She doesn't like men. Umm, she loves women."

I almost dropped a glass. "And you are all right with Chris being there?"

"No big deal. He is a grown man, and he has to learn how to take care of himself somehow."

"Well, I want to talk to him. Where is he staying? Is it close by?"

"Yeah, it's just down the hill. Chris is living with Marci. Now I hear Bruce coming in. Let's not talk about any of this in front of him, okay?"

My knees were weak, and I sat down at the table and buried my head in my hands.

"Oh, Lord," I whispered in a prayer.

Bruce came in with a big smile and hugged my neck.

"Mom, are you already asking the blessing?"

I looked up and smiled back at him. "Something like that." I stood and hugged him. "You hungry?"

* * * * *

I enjoyed my time with my son and Katie. As the evening wore on, we talked about a lot of things but not once about Chris. The clock was striking seven o'clock when I got up to leave. I needed to get home, and it would take me about thirty minutes to get there. We said our good nights, and they walked me to my car.

"Be safe now and hurry back to see us soon."

I was on my way down the hill, turning right, and there was Marci's house. It looked dark. Eerie shadows streaked across the house as the wind blew leaves on the trees in the light of the full moon. I couldn't tell if anyone was home because the windows were covered with dark blankets instead of curtains. I drove by slowly, but I didn't see Chris's car anywhere. I could hear a couple of dogs howling. There was something haunting about that place, and my grandson Chris was living there. It was a chilling thought.

I wasn't sure what my next move might be, but it is always "pray first." I really just wanted to go to that house, find Chris, and tell him to get out of there and go home. I was not looking forward to meeting Marci.

About a week had passed, and I was back to visit with Bruce and Katie. We finally talked about Chris, and they seemed okay with things. Chris had been back to their house and picked up some of his personal belongings. He seemed very pleased at being a driver for Marci, and at least, he was doing it on his own. He had a place to stay, and he was making some spending money. Marci lived close enough that they could keep an eye on Chris's comings and goings.

As I left to go home, I noticed Chris's car in Marci's driveway. I hesitated for a few minutes and then parked my car and walked up to the back door. When I knocked, a lot of little dogs came barking to alert everyone that someone was there. Chris came to the door.

"Grandma, why are you here? What's going on?" He was munching on a big sandwich and had his mouth full. He didn't ask me in; he just stood there, looking very surprised.

"I was about to ask you the same thing," I replied. "Can I come in?"

"Well, tell me what's going on, Grandma. I was just grabbing a bite to eat, and then, I was planning to take off. I need to run some errands for Marci."

"Is she here, Chris? I would really like to meet her. Are you going to make me stand out here all night?"

"Oh, sorry, Grandma, but she is sleeping, and I really have to get going. Maybe next time, when you come to see Mom and Dad, I can let Marci know that you want to meet her. I'll tell her you came by tonight." He fumbled for his car keys and pulled the door closed behind him.

"Chris," I said as we walked to my car, "I really don't have a good feeling about you living here like this."

He hugged me around the shoulder. "Aww, Grandma, you always worry about things too much. You ought to be proud of me. I am making it on my own. I guess I am finally taking some responsibility. Try not to worry."

"But, Chris, what kind of place is this? What kind of person is Marci?"

"Now, Grandma," he softened his voice, "I am fine, life is good, but it is getting dark, and I don't want you out driving in the country after dark. You need to get headed home. I don't want to have to worry about you. I will be calling you, and we can talk then. Okay? You need to move your car so I can get out of the driveway."

He walked me to the car and closed the door for me.

"What kind of errand are you running, Chris? Where did you say you were going?"

"I just need to get to the drugstore for Marci before it closes." He gave me a peck on the cheek. "You'd better get going. Bye, Grandma." He walked toward his car, and I pulled away.

I still had this eerie feeling that something still wasn't right.

Later that night, after I had read my Bible and was praying, I asked God to put a covering of protection over Chris. I asked God to show me a way that I could understand His will in this situation. After I went to bed, I had trouble sleeping. I was restless, tossing, turning, and waking up several times. Each time I awoke, I prayed again, but I got no answers.

Memories and thoughts filled my head.

I recalled how Bruce had discovered his first wife, Trilla, Chris's mother, cheating on him and the heartache and sorrow that caused. Chris had been brought up in church. He lived with me on several occasions before his dad had met and married Katie. Chris was only three years old. The custody battle was a tough one. Chris stayed with his mother during the court proceedings, and I recalled praying out to God fervently every day that He would intercede and that Chris would be allowed to be raised by Bruce. I knew we had entered into a family nightmare. Trilla was very beautiful, and it seemed every man wanted her body. Eventually, her secrets were revealed when her affair with a coworker of Bruce exploded. It broke a lot of hearts, and our concerns were for Chris. I knew that in our state of North Carolina, it would be difficult for a father to gain custody of a small child, even though he was the best parent for Chris. I cried out bitter tears and desperate prayers to a God who knew everything.

Toward the end of the custody proceedings, Trilla brought Chris home to Bruce, saying that she couldn't stand to hear him crying day and night for his daddy, and she would sign any papers necessary for Bruce to have full custody; but she wanted to retain visiting privileges. That was exactly what she did, and I knew that God had worked in His mysterious ways once again. I felt certain that God wanted us to bring Chris up in a Christian home. Bruce and Chris lived with me for about a year before he began to spend any time with his friends again. Those were happy days.

I finally drifted off into a peaceful sleep.

The next morning, I felt much better but had a nagging feeling bothering me, and I still wanted to see Marci. In my heart, I had peace knowing that, in God's time, it would happen.

Our meeting came only a few short weeks later. I was going to visit Bruce and Katie when passing by Marci's house. I noticed her outside in the backyard. She had a fire going and had been burning some trash in a big metal trash can. I saw Chris's car wasn't there, and I started not to stop but changed my mind. I pulled into the driveway, parked my car, and took a deep breath, wondering just what I was doing and what did I expect.

Marci threw up her hand to motion for me to come on in. As the wind shifted, I could barely see where to step with the billows of smoke burning my nose and eyes. When I finished fanning the smoke away, Marci was standing before me.

She was petite, had an amazing figure, and her hair was short, naturally curly, and very black. She was wearing jeans and a red shirt tied together at her waist. She was holding a large stick which she pulled along the ground behind her.

"Hey." She looked at me as she came closer. "You're Micki, Chris's grandmother, right?"

"Yes." I smiled back. "And you must be Marci?"

"The one and only." She laughed a hearty laugh as she put the stick in front of her and pushed it into the ground and rested her hands on it. She was in front of me now, and she didn't look, at all, as I had imagined her. She appeared to be very pleasant in her early forties. Her green eyes shining through lush long black lashes, very red lipstick, a great tan, and blushing pink cheeks. She looked like a very normal person and someone who took pride in herself.

"Sorry, I missed you the last time you came by. Chris told me about it. So what's up? You going to visit Bruce and Katie?"

"Yes, I saw you out here and figured it would be a good time to meet you." I tried to seem comfortable as I spoke. "I see you've been working in your yard."

"Just trying to burn some of this brush and sticks. You know, I think that Chris is a very fine young man."

"Oh, he is," I responded. "You know, he is his grandmother's pride and joy. I was a little concerned about him moving out from his home."

"Well, he has a long story to tell about that. I'm just lucky that he knocked on my door. He wanted to know if I knew of any place he might stay until he found a job, so I offered to take care of both of those things."

"Really?" I questioned her, "Just exactly what does he do for you?"

"Oh, don't get me wrong." She twisted her red lips. "I really need him around here. You see, I have my own truck but no driver's license, so he runs my errands for me and takes me anywhere that I need to go. I'm able to give him a place to stay and a little cash too."

"How did you lose your driver's license?"

"Oh," she said laughingly, "I guess I was just a bad girl. Would you like to go inside?"

"No, maybe next time. I need to go on over to see Bruce and Katie. They are expecting me. Be sure to let Chris know that we met each other today. I will try to stop by for a visit soon."

Back in my car, I was puzzled. I thought to myself, *She seems happy—comfortable to be around. Maybe I misjudged her, but still, the brooding feel of evil and demonic displays around her was a feeling I couldn't shake. Puzzled, I wondered how someone like her could enjoy a life like that.*

The following three weeks, I spent hours praying and seeking the will of God for Chris. I prayed for wisdom to know if there was anything I could actually do.

On a cold Saturday morning, I was on the dirt road again. As I approached Marci's house. I noticed that Chris was not there. His car was gone. I pulled into the drive and walked through the iron gate with a monster head on it. The dogs were barking before I even made it to the porch. After a few short knocks, Marci opened the door.

"Hey, come on in. Sorry if it feels a little cold in here, but I have to use small heaters. My furnace is on the blink."

The house was dimly lit with a few small lamps and some candles burning. The little dogs were jumping and growling around my feet until Marci commanded them to be quiet. I sat down on the soft worn couch and looked around. A painted pentagram hung on the wall; a statue of some creature sat in the corner. I turned to look at Marci.

"Well, Marci, how long have you been living here?"

"Uhmm, I guess about four years now. The place needs a lot of work, but I do what I can. I guess Chris told you that I'm on disability. That's the only income I actually have."

"No, he didn't. We haven't talked much lately. I thought I should check on him."

I wondered how she could keep up her house, own a truck, and pay Chris to run around for her.

"Well, he is just dandy," she exclaimed and lit a cigarette. "You don't mind if I smoke, do you?"

We chatted for a while, getting to know each other better. She had a solo cup beside of her chair, and occasionally, she would sip from it. We talked about Chris, Bruce, and Katie and how she was glad they had moved into the neighborhood. She didn't have many friends. She opened up with a lot of her personal stories, and I was very interested. When she asked about my life, I had the opportunity to tell her.

"First of all, I love the Lord Jesus. I am a child of God. I have been widowed and remarried now to Charles who is the love of my life."

She squirmed around a little, then moved onto the couch to sit beside of me.

With flashing green eyes and a taut chin, she began speaking with an almost hateful tone.

"Well, let me tell you about the love of my life! A beautiful woman—Renee—who filled every desire of my aching heart. We lived together for almost fourteen years, and then, God took her away from me. God snuffed out her life with cancer and, at the same time, destroyed everything that I had to live for." Her tone became angry. She raised her voice as she stood up, waving her arms in the air with a hateful look on her face. "I miss her every day. I will never forget her. How could any God ever do such an unforgivable thing? That is something I would like to know!" she yelled at me.

"I am so sorry for your loss, Marci, and I don't have all of the answers, but the God I serve is a God of love and the mender of broken hearts."

"Yeah, right."

"I know you are hurting and bitter, but there is hope and healing for you."

"Well, you know, Micki, things are just a little too far gone for me. I used to believe in a God like you do. I went to church with my mom, but now, my entire family is against me, and I haven't talked to them in a very long time." She was much calmer now as she stood up and stretched as if she had been sleeping.

"I am sorry if I said too much to you. After all, my problems are not your problems." She clicked her tongue in her mouth. "I will let Chris know that you stopped by."

That was my clue to leave. I stood up close to her. I could smell the alcohol on her breath.

"Marci, I am sorry if I upset you. That wasn't my intention at all. Would it be okay if I came by another day for a short visit?"

"Of course." She looked down to the floor and back up at me. "Whatever turns you on, lady. I could always use some company."

Marci walked me to the door. The dogs were yelping again, and I wondered if I had just made a mess of things.

Another month went by, and when I went for another visit with Bruce and Katie, I didn't stop or even look toward Marci's house. I was sure she didn't really want me to visit again, but it bothered me. A feeling of conscience that maybe I had failed—failed Chris, failed Marci, failed God.

* * * * *

Katie and Bruce were happy and had their home decorated with their Christmas tree and beautiful gifts already wrapped for the big day. Christmas was only two weeks away, and I had finally finished all of my shopping. Now, it was a time to relax and enjoy the company of my kids. I was pleasantly surprised when Chris dropped in.

"Hey, Grandma, how have you been? I haven't seen you in a long time." He gave me a hug and sat down beside me. "Hey, Mom and Dad, looks like you are ready for Christmas. How about you, Grandma? Are you tuckered out from spending all of your money?"

I laughed. "Now, Chris, you know the presents under my tree always say, 'Don't open before Christmas,' and that goes for you too."

He walked over to the tree and began looking at the gifts.

"Could one of these be for me?"

Katie exclaimed, "You put that down, big boy, you just have to wait."

It was a beautiful Saturday, and I was able to spend several hours with all three of them. When Chris started talking about Marci, I asked him how she was. He told us that she had been down in the dumps during December.

"However, she did put up a small Christmas tree on a table so the dogs wouldn't tear it up, with no presents under it. I was thinking about buying a present for her."

"That sounds like a thoughtful thing to do, Chris. Why don't you invite her to the church Christmas play?"

"Oh, I doubt that she would go, but I guess it wouldn't hurt to ask."

To everyone's surprise, Chris and Marci showed up for the Christmas play on Sunday night. I was happy to see her and asked them to sit with me. Marci was well dressed and rather comfortable during the program, but when they started the Nativity scene, she got up and walked outside. I followed her.

By the time I found her, she was smoking and leaning against the wall of the Fellowship Building.

"Marci, are you all right? It's freezing cold out here, let's go back inside."

"Nothing's wrong, I just had a sudden urge to smoke. You go back in. I will be there soon."

I went back inside for the closing of the program, and while I was congratulating the cast, Chris and Marci drove away.

Christmas Eve was a big celebration at my house; all of the family would gather for dinner and gifts. Chris wanted to invite Marci, and of course, I said yes. It was the first time that Marci had ever been in my house. She joined in with the family as we gathered around the piano, singing songs. She laughed a lot and enjoyed the great Christmas feast we all shared. I noticed when we asked God's blessing, she bowed her head and closed her eyes.

I prayed to myself, "God, show me the way."

Then, it was time to open the gifts. Everyone was so excited and tore into the gifts as they were given out one by one. Chris gave Marci a beautiful pair of earrings. She was overjoyed but pleasantly surprised when she also received gifts from Bruce, Katie, and me and Charles.

"What? All of you bought me gifts? This necklace is absolutely beautiful. *Oh*, I love this sweater, my favorite color."

When she opened my gift, she exclaimed, "Just what I needed—a new robe and bedroom slippers too. Oh, thank you. It is so thoughtful, thanks to all of you." She looked around the room with tears in her eyes. "I never dreamed all of you would buy me a gift." She sniffed. "I am so surprised! But I never bought any of you anything. I'm so sorry. I just haven't celebrated Christmas in a very long time."

"Just don't you worry about it," we all chimed in together.

"Anyway, you are almost like family to us." Chris brushed a tear from her eyes. "We have a lot to celebrate, and I'm going to read the Christmas story now."

As Chris read from the Bible about the birth of Jesus, I noticed that tears were still forming in Marci's eyes. Bruce and Katie left a little early while Chris and Marci still munched on some of the cookies. As they were preparing to leave, Marci stood at the door, looking at me.

"I have thoroughly enjoyed everything tonight. Your house is beautifully decorated, and I am very happy to have shared this time with you."

"We enjoyed having you here, Marci. You are free to come by anytime." I reached over and gave her a hug. "I hope we can get together often."

As our friendship began to grow, I had confidence that God was working in His own way and in His own time.

* * * * *

It was spring, and everything was in bloom. When I visited Marci on several of my visits, I asked her why she had all of those ugly things on her fence. She explained to me that she felt like it helped keep creeps away from her home. I told her that one of those things was a false god, and I'd just like to throw it away. She said I could do whatever I wanted with it, and as I walked to my car, I picked it up and trashed it. Marci got the hint. The next visit with her, I discovered that her wrought-iron fence was clear of everything; she had taken down the dark sheets over her windows and allowed light to come through her bedroom windows. She even came to church with Chris on a few occasions.

* * * * *

One summer night, Chris called me in a panic.

"Grandma, you've got to come here, quick! Something is wrong with Marci, she is acting so strange. She is snarling—growling even. She is lying on the couch, squirming and moving uncontrollably."

"Did you call 911? Is she sick?"

"No, Grandma, she's been drinking, and it's more than that. It is evil. When I tried to help her, she started clawing me like an animal. Come quick, come quick, she needs your help."

"Just leave her alone, Chris, I am on my way."

When I got there, I found Marci still lying on the couch in a fetal position. When I called out to her, chills ran down my spine as she answered me in a low, growling voice. It was not Marci's voice, and I knew it was a demon speaking. I began to plead to the blood of Jesus, and the voice grew intense.

"Leave me alone! Get away from me!" She began clawing at me.

The Holy Spirit took control, and I heard myself saying, "You lying devil, I come against you in the name of the Lord Jesus Christ, and you have no place here. Let her go."

"No! No! I won't." Her eyes were staring at me now, green and wicked. Chris was cowering in the corner of the room. As Marci began to act like some kind of cat creature and started to claw at me, I slapped her face as hard as I could.

"Oh yes, you will, you lying spirit. I said to let her go in Jesus Name, and you have to obey."

I could feel the victorious spirit of Jesus fill the room.

Marci stretched out stiffly on the couch and began to breathe normally.

"Micki, when did you get here? What's going on?" she whimpered.

I explained to her what had happened and told her that an evil spirit had taken control of her body, that alcohol had allowed her to weaken, and that the devil desired to have her. She was shaking from head to toe. I asked her if anything like this had ever happened before, and she said she couldn't remember, but she thought that it had. I told her that the spirit would come back and that she needed to give her heart and soul to Jesus Christ.

"I know I do," she said in a trembling voice. "But how? He will never forgive me. You have no idea of the things I have done."

"Yes, He will." I explained, "If you are ready and willing to serve Him, He loves you, and He can help you. Just ask Him to forgive you right now, right here, please."

"I can't, I can't." She sobbed. "I just can't. I am not good enough."

"You don't have to be good enough, Marci. His love covers a multitude of sin. He wants to forgive you and give you a new life."

"I can't not yet," she pleaded. "I am going to quit drinking and start going to church more. I will make myself a better person." She hugged me. "I'm all right now, Micki. Thank you for coming. I'm going to make some strong coffee, and I don't plan to go back to sleep tonight. I will go to church with you tomorrow night, I promise."

Marci kept her promise and came to church Sunday night. She tried to take part by singing and listening to the minister's message. When the altar call was given, she didn't move. I gathered with some of the people around the altar, praying for each other, then I heard a familiar sound. A low, slow growling voice. I turned to look at Marci. She was writhing in some kind of pain, and the voice was speaking.

"I won't come out, I won't!"

Immediately, the minister and several of the men in the congregation gathered around Marci. The preacher began to pray as he laid hands on Marci's head.

"All of the congregation needs to close those eyes and cry out to God for this woman. Satan, I command you, in the name of Jesus Christ our Lord, to get out of her now, and let this woman go!"

The preacher continued to pray fervently as the others around him and the entire congregation began to call out for deliverance for Marci. The enemy tried to resist releasing her, but he could not stand the power of God and faith that filled the room. In a moment, he was gone, and Marci was set free from demonic powers. She stood up weakly and made her way to the altar to accept Jesus as her savior.

The days that followed were different; Marci was different. She was happy and visited with me many times as I helped lead her into more victories. God had moved in her life. I was only the vessel He used to get to her. All the glory and honor go to Him.

She still had things to overcome; she took down the horoscopes, the pentagram, and she found her old Bible and began reading it. She got rid of the books and video tapes of murders and monsters. She began to watch some Christian programs on television and found strength to be strong in the Lord. Her life was changed.

She did become a part of our family. Chris stayed with her, and he brought his girlfriend, Cassi, to visit with Marci many times.

About two years had passed when Chris called me again in a panicked voice.

"Grandma! Grandma! Help us, please. Come quick!"

He hung up before I could ask him what was happening. I wondered if things were bad again, but I had confidence that Marci had stayed true to God and to her new life.

As I rounded the curve toward Marci's house, I passed the ambulance with sirens blasting. I ran to Chris who had his head in his hands, sobbing.

"Chris, what happened? I got here as quickly as I could."

"Marci was lying on the couch, watching television and eating something. She hadn't been feeling well. Cassi and I had just walked out into the yard when I heard Marci making a choking sound."

"Oh no! Were you able to help her?"

"I tried, Grandma, I really tried, but then, she started throwing up and couldn't breathe. That's when she passed out."

"Oh, Chris, what did you do?"

"I yelled for Cassi to call 911 while I tried to clear Marci's passageway for air and then gave her CPR until the ambulance arrived. She was breathing again, Grandma, but I think she is dying." He sobbed.

I hugged him, and he laid his head on my shoulder, weeping.

"Chris, I'm so sorry. We all love Marci so much. We just have to pray that she will be all right, and we need to go to the hospital too. What about her family? Has Marci ever told you how to reach them?"

"Just her aunt Betty, she has her number in her phone. It is still in the house by the couch."

We contacted Betty, and she said she would call Marci's mother and her family. They would be going to the hospital right away. They would give us a report as soon as they learned anything. There was no use for us to go to the hospital, but she would call us soon. I had never met any of Marci's family, so we waited for the call. It was late that night when we got word that Marci was brain dead. She had been unconscious too long, and it didn't look good. They had her on life support. The next morning, I made my way to the hospital. I met Marci's mother and her aunt Betty. Marci was still on life support when I was able to see her. I put my hands on her as tears trickled down my cheeks. I prayed for her, for peace, and that God would work a miracle for Marci. She was so cold, and there was no response.

I sat down on a chair as her mother and Aunt Betty came back in and sat down.

"What is the doctor saying? Is everything going to be all right for Marci?"

Della, Marci's mom, a heavyset woman, settled into a recliner. I remembered that she and Marci had not shared much of a relationship.

"No, the doctors say she is brain dead, and there is no reason to keep her here." She coughed. "So they will be in here in a few minutes to take her off of life support."

"Already?" I questioned, "Are you sure there is no chance for her survival?"

"Even if she lived, she wouldn't be able to function as a normal person. It is just better this way." Della continued, "We did what we had to do."

"I have always cared about Marci," Aunt Betty spoke softly. "She really had a hard life."

"But you do know that Marci was a Christian now, don't you? She was faithful in church and such a good friend to me and my family. We loved her so much." I brushed away my tears; my heart was aching at the very fact they weren't giving her any more time. I had heard of people being brain dead and then recovering, but it wasn't going to happen to Marci. After they took her off of life support, I stood by her bedside. She looked so peaceful, just like she was asleep. She never breathed. I touched her cheek and said my goodbyes.

"Please, let me know of the arrangements and if there is anything I can do to help."

"We will." Della patted me on the back. "We will have to go over and clean out her house, and someone will pick up her truck."

I felt a tremble run through me as I remembered I would have to tell Chris and the rest of our family.

We sent flowers and attended the funeral services. In the months to follow, we often spoke of Marci and what she meant to us.

In late Autumn, I was getting out my winter clothes for the season, when I noticed a book lying on the top shelf of my closet. I pulled it down to look at it. It was a book about the life story of Johnny Cash; Marci had given it to me a long time ago. I just never got around to reading it. I flipped through the pages and pulled out a folded piece of paper. I guessed she had marked some pages when she read it. I unfolded the paper to discover it was a letter. My knees felt weak, so I sat down to read it. It was from Marci. Tears flowed down my cheeks as I read.

> *My name is Marci, and this is a letter to anyone who ever sees it. I just want to thank God for saving me, and I want to thank God for sending Micki into my life. She has meant more to me than anyone I have ever met. I know she loves God and serves Him with all of her heart. By the grace of God and her life and witness, my life has been changed. Thank you, God, my heavenly Father.*

So many times, we never know what may lie ahead when God decides to put you in someone's life. He expects us to lean on Him and trust His ways to follow the direction He may be leading us in.

When the chains of Satan are broken, deliverance brings freedom, joy and peace.

11

Best Friends Forever

We had started pastoring a small church in South Carolina. I was eager to make new friends. Our congregation was very small, so I knew I had to work hard inviting people to church. My boys were small; Ricky was in the head-start program, and Bruce was a second grader. I knew they would also need to make new friends—other children to play with.

I was out in my yard, planting some flowers, when Flo and her two children, Cami and Eddie, came down the street, walking past my house. I threw up my hand and sounded a cheerful hello. They turned and looked at me, then put their heads down and kept walking. They never said a word. I stood there as she pulled her kids close and muttered something to them. I was a little shocked; I was not accustomed to being ignored when I was just trying to be neighborly. Her children looked to be about the same age as Ricky and Bruce. I decided not to let it bother me. It was late spring, and I eventually learned that they regularly visited Flo's mother who lived just down the street from me. I noticed them several more times, but I wasn't outside.

One weekend, while I was sweeping my porch, I saw them coming down the road again. I put my broom down and walked to the fence. When they were close enough, they were trying, once again, to pretend not to see me.

"Hey," I yelled out, "I just wanted to invite you and your kids to our church. We are going to have a kids crusade when school is out for summer vacation. I know they would enjoy it."

This time, I could hear what she said to her children.

"Don't pay her any attention." She pulled her daughter by her arm. "Cami, don't wave at her. That old woman's crazy."

Cami had turned to look at me and had started to wave, but Flo brought her hand down quickly.

I thought silently, *What is her problem? I certainly am not crazy, and I am not old.*

I decided not to bother them again. Weeks followed, and I saw them many times walking slowly down the road to her moms, and then back again to their house. Finally, school was out, and I had my hands full, taking care of my boys. It seemed like they wanted something to eat every two hours, they wanted to go for ice cream, or to a ball game, the park, or whatever it would take to keep me busy.

Every time I noticed Flo and her children walking down the road, there was a tugging at my heart. Why couldn't I just leave it alone? I knew there was something drawing me toward them. It was the Holy Spirit urging me for some reason. I argued to myself.

She made it pretty clear to me that she was not interested in anything I have to say. The kids crusade will be soon, and I would love for them to be there. A mother should not deny her children the opportunity to have fun and learn about Jesus at the same time. But, Lord, I can only push so far. "Push," the words echoed in my head. PUSH—*Pray Until Something Happens!* That is exactly what I did.

About two weeks had passed; one evening, after dinner, my boys and I were in the front yard. They were playing ball, and I was cheering them on. Flo and her children were returning home and, once again, walking past my house. My boys jumped up and ran to the fence.

"Hey, Eddie, you live around here?" Bruce shouted out. "Wanna play some ball?"

Flo couldn't hold Eddie as he ran toward the fence.

"Hey, Bruce." Eddie grinned. "I didn't know this was your house."

"Yeah, I'd like to play some ball with you. Is that your little brother, Ricky?"

Bruce and Ricky ran to open the gate as Eddie turned to his mom.

"Mom, this is Bruce and Eddie. Bruce was in my class this year. Can I stay for a while?"

Flo was at the fence, and Cami was asking if she could play too. I walked over to speak to them.

"My name is Micki. Why don't you let them play for a while? My husband pastors the Crossroads Community Church. Do you know where it is? I thought, maybe, you and your kids could come and visit with us one Sunday."

"I'm called Flo. I'm sorry if we seemed rude before. I just don't want my kids to get in the habit of talking to strangers. Yes, I know where your church is, but my husband and I go to First Baptist downtown, when we go."

I smiled as I looked at her straight auburn hair and soft brown eyes. Her face was kind. She looked like a wholesome country girl—a picture of health. A mother who believed in protecting her children.

"That's great. We are having a kids crusade next week. Now that school is out, maybe you could bring your kids. It will be in the mornings, Monday through Thursday at ten o'clock."

A bright smile crossed her face.

"I'll think about it. I'm sure they would enjoy it. Looks like they are having fun now. That Cami thinks she is one of the boys. They better watch out. She will hit a ball over this fence."

We stood at the gate, laughing and watching the kids play for a while, then I invited Flo to come in and sit with me. I knew she wasn't about to leave the kids and go on down the road. We sat on the steps, and I poured her a glass of lemonade. She was likeable, funny, and very relaxed. She told me about her mother and where she lived. Every now and then, she would call out to the kids to be careful and not to throw the ball toward the house. I enjoyed her company, and to my surprise she seemed to like me too. Before they left, she said she would have Eddie and Cami at the kids crusade. That is just what she did.

I met her husband, Rob, and introduced them to Bill. They seemed to hit it off right away, talking about fishing and where the best places were to take Rob's boat. Flo and Rob sat in the back with the other parents while the crusade brought life and laughter to the children. The action Bible stories were a perfect way to get the true message across.

Afterward, we had refreshments on the picnic tables outside and spent more time with Flo and Rob, along with some of the other parents. Rob wasn't able to come every day, but Flo and the children showed up for every service.

On Sunday morning, I was happy to see Flo, Rob, Eddie, and Cami come through the doors to join us for service.

Happy times followed those early beginnings. Flo and I took our children everywhere together. We went to the park, museums, picnics, and anywhere else we could think of. She took me to meet her mother, Bonnie, a blessed and beautiful woman with soft white hair and big brown eyes. Bonnie may have been frail and weak, but she could talk up a storm. We were mesmerized by her wisdom and stories of her life. I met everybody in Flo's families and kin. They seemed like my own family. It was comforting, especially when my parents lived in another state.

In the months that turned into years, Flo and I became the best of friends. She became a strong pillar in our church, and when I had any problems, she was always there for me.

Eventually, the time came for us to make another move, and we accepted a pastoral role in a small country town in North Carolina. Flo and I made many phone calls to each other and a lot of visits too. Through these years, she and Rob had two more children—another girl and another boy. When she came to tell me she was expecting her third child, she insisted that I would have to name him, but told me that whatever name I chose wouldn't really matter because he would be called Mickey—after me. On the day of his birth, he was named Michael, and to this day, he is still called Mickey. I had agreed with her that I would be the godmother of her children, and she would always be there for my children.

Years passed, and I lived in a lot of different places, but it didn't matter whether I was in North Carolina, South Carolina, Florida, or any place in the world; I knew I always had a true friend back in South Carolina.

When Rob became very sick and near the point of death, I prayed with them. One night, when I had called her to see how he was doing, he told her to give him the phone. I was so happy he was able to talk.

"Hey, Rob, are you feeling any better?"

He spoke in a very weak voice. "I love you," he whispered and then kissed the phone.

Tears ran down my face as he gave the phone back to Flo.

It was only a few weeks after that he passed away. One of his last requests was that I sing his favorite song at his funeral. It was a difficult day, but it was a comfort to the family as I sang "I Want to Stroll Over Heaven with You."

Flo was a very strong person, but later in life, she had a lot of medical problems. I went to be with her as much as I could. My last visit with her was at the hospital, and I knew it wouldn't be long before she passed on to glory. I was planning to go back on the next Saturday when I got the call that she had passed away. I went to be with her and the family. It was hard losing my best friend after over fifty years. My heart flooded with memories and love. I thanked God for knowing her and for putting her and her family in my pathway of life. When they told me her last wish was for me to preach at her funeral, I wasn't sure I would physically be able too.

When the family gathered at the funeral home and friends came to view her, my knees were so weak I didn't think I could even walk into the chapel. God gave me the strength to go in, to bring comfort to the family I loved, and to preach the Word of God to all of the people gathered there to say goodbye. The text of my message was from the story of David when his baby died. He couldn't do anything about his baby passing, but he told them that he could go to him. I gave hope to all of those people there that Flo's passing was not the end; it was her beginning, and we could all go to her. Our Lord and Savior had made a way for us to be together again. I knew she was rejoicing with Jesus and Rob, and she would be waiting for all of us to get there.

My precious friend on this Earth would someday be my friend through all eternity.

Love for one another can be the secret to much happiness and a lifetime friendship.

12

Adventure at the Volcano

When my sister, Becky, my niece, Jenny, and I made a trip to Costa Rica, we had many adventures. We were guests of our missionary friends, Kim and Jonathan. We participated in all of their worship with the young people there; we did street ministries, puppet plays about Jesus and His wonderful plan of salvation at the schools in San Jose, we helped with an Indian community project, front-porch Sunday-school stories, and were serenaded by a local group of teenagers at night.

We also ventured into the rain forest and the cloud forest. During our walking visit in the rain forest with our guide, we were looking at various trees and also watching for snakes and other wildlife. I had seen people doing that on television before and was sure I would never be in a place like that, but there I was. Becky and I had found one small snake which we pointed out to our guide. It was no bigger than our little finger and was curled up close to our path. He took one look and advised us to stay away from it. He called it an eyelash viper and explained that if it bit us, we would not have made it back to our camp alive. We would have been dead in less than fifteen minutes.

We took the chair lift ride through the rain forest. It was exciting to go so quietly through the air so that the monkeys and other wildlife would not be disturbed. Beautiful was a way to describe it, until a spider decided to ride on my chair lift with me, but his visit was cut short, and I could relax again.

That spider was nothing like the one we nicknamed "The Itsy Bitsy" which hopped onto our car coming from Jaco Beach. That spider was larger than my hand spread wide open. All of the windows were instantly raised in the car to keep the spider out. He wouldn't go away. He ran from the windshield around all of the windows and then to the rear window and back to the windshield again for almost thirty miles. All of the screaming and squeals are unforgettable. Finally, after we were back to our motel, Jonathan (the brave man) was able to knock the spider off of the car, and we ran to our room.

Of all the things that happened, and there are a lot more that I could tell you of, the trip to the volcano was very special. There were seven of us that made the trip to the volcano—me; my sister, Becky; my niece, Jenny; our missionary friend, Kim; and her two daughters and a friend of hers who was also our guide. All girls.

On the drive up the steep mountain, Kim pointed out where all the rocks and boulders were still lying from the last time that the volcano had erupted a few years ago. It was still considered an active volcano. I was just so excited that it didn't really occur to me what she meant by active.

When we finally made it to the top of the mountain and the bottom of the volcano. We parked the car and started the climb to the top of it. Finally, I couldn't believe I was actually looking into the mouth of a real volcano. It was a long way down to the center, and I could see what looked like a smooth light-green-colored lake at the bottom. The wonders of our Creator were made so wonderfully real to me.

Finally, we started back down the steep mountain in the car. The brakes started burning, and they were about to burn out. We had to stop and let the brakes cool before we could get down the mountain. The seven of us got out of the car and went into a beautiful meadow where we sat and talked for a while, sharing testimonies and stories of blessings and adventure. There were rocks and stones in various places of the meadow. We were looking at them and picking some of them up. I was thinking about the twelve stones that were placed on the Red Sea when God led the children of Israel through the parted waters. I also thought of other times when an altar of rocks or stones were built as a memorial for people to remember what God had done for them. As these thoughts were going through my mind, I said, "Let's build an altar to God for allowing us to be here without another eruption."

They all agreed, and we each took a good-sized rock and put them together to build an altar in memory of the place we would worship God. Then, we worshipped Him by singing and dancing around the rock. It was a beautiful praise service. We prayed to our Heavenly Father and thanked Him for allowing us to be there. We could feel His presence.

After some time, we were able to get back in the car and down the mountain. Of course, we were hungry after our adventure and went into a small café at the foot of the mountain. There was a television playing in Spanish, but when the news interrupted the program, Kim's eyes grew very big. She became very excited, and we asked her what was happening. She exclaimed to us that the news said there was a rumbling in the volcano we had just visited. I could see fear on her face, but I felt a very calm assurance come over me. I looked at the others and smiled.

"Oh, I just believe that was God shaking the ground to let us know He liked our worship and our memorial seven-rock altar."

To this day, I still feel in my heart that being on top of that mountain and worshiping our God was the most wonderful and amazing adventure of the entire trip.

The magnificent presence of God can be found anywhere.

My Personal Experiences with a Loving God

The following events occurred in my own personal life and with my family. I believe you will find them amazing, just as I have. We can never know what the future holds for us, whether joy, happiness, grief, or pain. It is likely that you will experience all of them. However, life is a journey and we must remember there is a power that protects us, a Christ who loves us, and a God who guides us. His ways are not our ways, and just when we think there is no way, God shows us that His way is the only way. If you will gently surrender to the will of God, things will definitely change. The results will be heartwarming, amazing, and sometimes miraculous. You don't need to have special abilities, talents, or experience. You just have to be willing and available, sincere and prayerful, having a desire to draw closer to God, and reach out to help others. What God has done for me, he wants to do for you. There is a power greater than you can imagine—a power that turns dreams into reality, which will change your lives and the lives of many others.

13

A Dream, a Passing, a Revelation

It was a cold and rainy night in late October when I sleepily crawled into my bed. There was a tender good-night kiss, and Bill folded his arms around me. He held me until I was sleeping soundly. I have always had very vivid dreams, but this night, my dreams turned into horrible nightmares.

In my dream, I saw my fourteen-year-old Ricky rushing to my bedside; he was visibly upset and spoke in an alarmed tone.

"Mom! Mom! Wake up, come quick. Bruce is dying. He's in here!"

"What, Ricky?" I was immediately on my feet and fell to my knees and, praying—actually, running on my knees—I followed him to the bathroom. That was where I saw Bruce; doubled over with his arms folded at his stomach. His eyes were tightly closed in pain, his face deathly white with bluish lips."

I cried out, "Oh, God! No!" I was still on my knees. I pulled Bruce's face up toward me and wrapped his limp body in my arms. I prayed fervently and in desperation.

"Oh, my God, Father, please, don't take my son away from me. God, please, have mercy and breathe life back into him. Oh, God, oh, God! He is my firstborn, flesh of my flesh. God, I cry out to You in mercy for my son."

Tears were flowing down my cheeks like torrents of rain; my heart was beating furiously. I looked at Bruce. His color was coming back. His eyelids were blinking; he looked at me and smiled. I knew God had answered this mother's prayer. Then, I woke up.

I was trembling from my head to my feet, my heart was pounding, and my pillow was soaked with my tears. I thought to myself, *Oh, thank you, God, it was only a dream.* But what a horrible dream it was. I got out of bed, drank a glass of water, and when I had finally quit shaking and calmed down, I went back to my bed and prayed a special prayer for Bruce.

Soon, I felt my eyes getting heavy and finally fell asleep again. I began to dream.

I dreamed I was asleep in my bed when I saw my seventeen-year-old Bruce come hastily into my bedroom. I sat up, startled, as I heard him say, "Come on, Mom, get dressed. We have to go the hospital. Ricky is dying!"

It felt as if my heart had stopped as I threw on my clothes, slipped on my shoes, and grabbed my coat. I was shaking from hearing that Ricky was in the hospital. Bruce wrapped me in his arms and explained that something had happened, and they had to rush Ricky to the hospital and that it was matter of life and death. Then, suddenly, we were opening the door to Ricky's room at the hospital. I saw my son, Ricky, lying quietly against a white pillow, but fear gripped me as I saw Ricky's face, whiter than the pillow. No monitors, no beeping sound, no oxygen, no life support, nothing. It was like he was already dead, and we were too late. I fell across his chest; I could still a hear a low heartbeat. An essence of agony, aches, and pains swept up inside of me from very deep down within. Blinding tears were gushing from my eyes. I was sobbing a prayer to God.

"Oh, God, oh, God, oh, God, this is my baby boy. He is a part of me, he is so young, and he loves You. Please, God, oh, please, God, don't let this happen, and don't take Ricky away from me. Please, God, I am begging You for his life. Send him back to me. Oh, God, raise him up," I pleaded.

I felt Ricky's hand patting my back. I looked into his bright-blue eyes and saw him smiling as he said, "Mom, I'm okay." As I laid my head again on his chest, I closed my eyes, and when I opened them again, I was in my bed.

My hands were wiping tears from my face, I was shaking and trembling, my gown was wet with tears, and my pillow was soaked.

It was another horrible dream. What could all of this mean? God, why would you let me have such vivid dreams about my sons dying? Why did this happen only minutes apart?

I was visibly shaken and disturbed. I was ever so thankful that they were only some nightmares and not reality. It was even harder for me to get back to sleep, but eventually, I was resting quietly again. I even had another dream, but it was not significant or disturbing. I dreamed about a small yellow house on a beach in Florida. I dreamed that Bill and I had bought it and planned to move back to Florida. We would retire there someday.

The next time I awoke, Bill was coming out of the bathroom. It was Sunday morning, and he had already taken his shower and was dressed for church. He had let me sleep in a little longer than usual.

"How did you sleep?" He smiled at me in his own cheery way.

I remembered the dreams—the horrible dreams of both my sons dying but didn't want to share those with anyone, then I thought about the yellow house on the beach.

"Oh, I had a dream last night that we were going to move back to Florida."

"Is that right?" He straightened his tie. He was standing at the foot of the bed, looking at me through the mirror.

"Yeah, it was a small house, but it was right on the beach."

"Sounds good to me." He grinned.

"But it was painted bright-yellow!" I chuckled.

Teasingly, he called back, "Oh, no! Not a yellow house. You have got to be kidding me."

We both laughed together, then he walked to the side of the bed where I was sitting. He stretched out his long arm to me and said sweetly, "Honey, one of these days, I am going to buy an airplane ticket as long as my arm, and we are going to travel everywhere you have ever wanted to go."

"Yeah." I smiled back at him. "The sooner the better."

"Well, you better start getting ready. We don't want to be late for church."

Before I could even stand up, Bill had walked into the open doorway to our hall when he threw both hands in the air and, with a long breath, said, "Whew," as he crumbled to the floor. I was at his side immediately, screaming, "Oh, God! Oh, God." I heard his breath leave him. "Whooshhh."

I dialed 911 for an ambulance. I put nitroglycerin under his tongue. I tried to do CPR while I called my dad and mom to come quickly. I was crying, my heart was pounding, and sobs came from somewhere deep inside of me. I prayed and prayed just like I had been praying in my terrible nightmares, but Bill was unresponsive. Somehow, my house filled up with people. I didn't remember calling my neighbors. Maybe they heard me crying and screaming. There was one man—a stranger—a big-bodied man with light-brown hair; he did CPR until the ambulance finally arrived. I had never seen this man before, and I never saw him again. The paramedics rushed into the scene, checked Bill over thoroughly, and covered his face with a sheet. Instantly, I uncovered his face.

"No, no, he is not dead. You have to take him to the hospital, please."

"Okay, ma'am, can you have someone meet us there for you?"

"Yes." Mom and Dad were on their way. Ricky had spent the night with his grandparents. Bruce was out of town.

I thanked the tall stranger for doing the CPR for such a long time. He told me that he did it for me because he knew Bill was already gone, and he didn't stop until the paramedics got there. Looking back at that time, I wonder if he was a messenger from God.

I rode in the ambulance to the hospital, the same hospital where I had just experienced my dream of Ricky dying a few short hours ago. I never noticed that they didn't use the sirens, and it never occurred to me that they were carrying Bill to the morgue.

I really don't remember much of what happened at the hospital. I don't remember getting out of the ambulance or seeing them take Bill out. I must have passed out. When I regained awareness, I was in a private waiting area. The doctors said Bill had suffered a massive heart attack, and that even if he had been in the surgery, they would not have been able to save him. Mom was sitting on one side of me, and Ricky was on the other side. They had gone to the morgue and identified Bill's body. My mom's big brown eyes looked softly at me as she whispered, "He's gone." I still couldn't believe it. Dad had taken off to my sister's house as she was also married to a Bill, and he thought she had called. I told Mom and Ricky about my two horrible dreams and that both of my boys had lived and how Bill was supposed to live too. *How could I go on without him? What could life possibly hold for me now? He was my rock!*

I can barely remember leaving the hospital, but Mom and Ricky were holding me up. I was so weak. I was thinking, *This is the most horrible night of my life. I'm sure I will wake up soon.*

But I didn't. Bill was really gone in a moment's breath. God had called him to glory. But I asked myself so many times after that, *God how could You let me have those horrible dreams and then take Bill away from me? Why didn't You heal him the way you healed my boys in my dream? Was it my fault?*

But I got no answer.

I could never put into words how I felt during those days of loss. The funeral, the friends, the flowers, the gravesite. The emptiness, the dreams that followed. God was my strength! My precious Mom and Dad were there for me. My wonderful sons, Bruce and Ricky, helping me through some of the toughest times of my life. It had happened so suddenly, and many times, I found myself wanting to ask God, "Why?" and other times, I would think of something that I needed to ask Bill as he was the only person that would know the answer to my questions, but he was not there. I felt so alone, I had so many questions, I was hurting like I had never hurt before in my life. Sometimes, it was difficult to even pray. I still could not understand why God would allow me to have those two dreams of both my sons dying and then, at the same time, letting Bill die in my arms. All of that pain—the nightmare, I just couldn't wake up from. I was still upset months after all of these happened. I recall vividly, one day, I was driving down a long country road, thinking and praying to myself again, and wondering about the events of that horrible night. At the beginning, I thought that God was being cruel to me for some strange reason, but I knew in my heart God is not cruel; He is a God of love and protection.

"So why, God, why did You allow this to happen this way? Nightmares of my sons dying just before You knew that Bill was going to go to his eternal home that morning?"

"I wanted you to remember that you still have your sons." The voice of God filled the air; God spoke to me. His voice was not a soft-spoken whisper in my head as He had often spoken to me before, but it was an audible voice speaking loudly.

I was overwhelmed. Tears sprang to my eyes.

"Oh, Father God, You did it for me! You allowed this to happen so I would not feel like I had lost everything. Bill was in his own way, my world, but so are my sons, and You didn't take my sons. Oh, how horrible it would have been if I had lost all of them. You were preparing me for Bill's passing. Oh, God, I'm so sorry. I just didn't understand. Forgive me my, Heavenly Father. Thank You for loving me that much."

* * * * *

My Mom had been the most comforting emotional support for me. She was so caring. She was so gentle and wanted to help me get over the feeling of so much loss. Ricky and I had moved back home with Mom and Dad. Bruce decided to room with one of his friends. Mom even slept with me for a while. Bill and I had often said that we both hoped when it came our time to go, we would go together. God had chosen to take only him, and my heart longed to see him.

14

More Acts of God's Mercy to Me

Tricked by the Devil

One night, I had not yet gone to sleep, tossing and turning and so uncomfortable, so I started praying. I could feel the Spirit of the Lord as I was crying out to Him. I felt another strange sense in my room and saw a small flame of fire on the right side of my bed. It was just at my mattress's level, floating in the air. I was alarmed and sat straight up. Then, there was another small flame, and then another; they were slowly circling my bed. I watched as they reached the foot of my bed, still circling. I, then, heard the voice of my enemy—the devil.

"Those are the flames of hell. You are going to see Bill burning in hell. He wasn't saved. He didn't make it. You are going to see for yourself." He was laughing wickedly. Although I couldn't see him, I covered my eyes. When I looked again, I saw the flames were now on the left side of my bed, almost fully circled.

"Oh, God!" I cried out. "This is not true. Please, God, I don't want to see anything."

Immediately, the small flames of fire disappeared. I was relieved until I heard the small still voice of God speak to me. "My precious child, those were cloven tongues of fire—the Holy Spirit."

I fell back onto my pillow.

"Oh, Father God. I am so sorry that I let fear overcome me. I let the devil trick me. Will you please do it again?"

Nothing happened, and I knew that I had missed my opportunity for a wondrous spiritual experience.

A Small Girl's Witness

My niece, Jessica, was three years old when Bill died. She had been to visit us many times, and she loved her uncle Bill.

Our family was attending a church cookout. I was following Dad's car with my car. Jessica was riding with them. This was a time before the seatbelt law, and she was on my mom's lap. Jessica started pointing to the sky, very excited.

"Look! Look!" she exclaimed, bouncing up and down on Mom's lap. "Look! Look! Look!"

Mom looked into the night sky but couldn't see anything. Jessica just kept up the excitement. Mom asked Dad, "Do you see anything up there? Why is she so excited?"

By now, Dad was looking too. Both of them were scanning the skies to find what Jessica was looking at.

Dad said, "I thought it might be a plane, but I don't see anything. Jessica, what do you see? Can you tell Grandpa what you see?"

Still pointing to the dark sky, Jessica replied with all the excitement that a three-year-old could have, "Jesus! Bill!"

My folks couldn't wait to share the story with me. God is so good. He chose a tiny child that could never make up something like this to bear witness to our hearts.

Choices

Mom was still my greatest comforter; she helped me to accept the loss I felt as part of God's will. Sometimes, at night, she would lie down beside me, hug me, and tell me that everything was going to be all right. One night, she fell asleep before I did. It was in the wee hours of the early morning when there was a strange feeling in the room. I sat up to see Jesus and Bill standing at the foot of my bed. Jesus, so radiant with such a wonderful look of love, was smiling at me. Then, I turned my eyes to Bill; he was standing there right in front of me. He appeared to be about thirty years old—so handsome, radiant, young, and healthy, smiling gently. He held out his hand and spoke to me.

"Micki, we are here now. Do you want to come with us?"

My heart leaped with joy and excitement at the thoughts of going to my final home. Just then, I looked at my precious mother; she was curled up and sleeping peacefully.

She looked so small, so tender. She had poured all of the love she had into helping me. How could I leave her now? How could I cause her so much pain?

Looking at her for a few moments, I turned my head back to them and said, *"I just can't leave yet."*

I knew I couldn't leave my mother that night, and I was given a choice. I pulled the covers gently over her frail body. When I looked back toward the foot of my bed, no one was there. Jesus and Bill were gone. You may think this was just a dream, but I am sure it was not. It was very real.

Close Encounters of a Kind God

After Bill's death, my emotions were unreal. I had so many things to take care of. We had so many flowers at the funeral I didn't quite know what to do with them. The beautiful stands of live flowers I left at the gravesite, but the artificial arrangements had to be put somewhere until I could do something with them. I hoped to always leave one on his grave every month. I instructed someone (I can't even remember who helped me) to take them to the office for storage. There was a hallway from the lobby to my office and Bill's office. Temporarily, until I could find a storage place for them, I had these arrangements very carefully lined up down the hall on the right and left sides, making a hallway of beautiful flowers from thoughtful people who had loved Bill.

It was late one evening, after dark, and I had to have some very important papers to take to the attorney. Bill had told me many times not to go to the office alone after dark. I never would have gone alone, but this night, I felt like I had to. If I drove all the way back to my parents' house, I would have to return early the next morning. It was about a thirty-mile round trip, and I was already exhausted. I decided I would go in and get the papers. Our office was nestled in a wooded area, quite a distance from the main road. I unlocked the door to the lobby and turned off the alarm. There was another door from the lobby into the office. Our office receptionist sat near the opening door to the office, but she had a glass window which was locked unless she chose to open it for our guest. I really hoped it had been left unlocked. When I discovered it was locked, and I could not open the inside door, I was almost in tears. Overwhelmed with stress and sorrow, I just put my head into my hands and leaned against the ledge in front of the receptionist window. I could feel big tears welling up in my eyes as I started talking to God.

"God, I know I'm not supposed to ask why, but I really do need some help getting into the offices. You know how important this is to me. Dear God, I am so stressed and so tired, please, help me."

I just leaned there in the deep silence of the room, wiping tears from my eyes and looking at the lock I couldn't reach through the window. In the silence, I heard something click. My heart froze, and my face grew hot while icy chills tingled up and down my spine. My first thoughts were that someone else was in the office with me, so I bolted for the outside doors. I wanted to get away as fast as I could. As I started to push the door open to leave, I stopped and looked around.

That really sounded like a door lock unlatched. God, did You unlock the inside door? I paused. *I know that I asked God to help me, and He is here with me. I can't leave this building until I find out for sure if He unlocked the door.*

Trembling, I walked back over to the inside door; it was unlocked! I was frightened and thankful at the same time. I flipped on the lights and walked down an aisle of beautiful flowers to my office. I quickly picked up the papers I needed and hurried out of the building.

In my car, I was still shaking a little. God had done a very special thing for me. There really was someone else in the office; it was God. He was with me, He heard my prayers, He saw my weeping spirit, and He unlocked the door and met my needs. What a wonderful God we serve. He promised to never leave us or forsake us.

When I look back at my life through these many years, there were several incidents where I could have died. There were probably even many more that I didn't know about, but here are a few of the things that happened to me.

The Invisible Shield of Mercy

Many years ago, as a young woman, I worked for a small loan company downtown. I had to park in a parking lot and use a back alley to go to the office. One afternoon, after leaving the office, I was walking down that back alley to my car. I was almost to the main street when a car came roaring around the corner and quickly turned into the alley, directly in my pathway. I froze in my tracks, unable to move before the expected impact. I remember seeing the panic-stricken face of the man driving the car. He was shocked as much as I was. It was inevitable that we would collide; then, just like that, an invisible shield or some sort of force field came between us. A moment was frozen in time. We were separated. His car stopped, and I was unharmed. That's the first incident that I can recall.

Jesus Took the Wheel

Another time, I was driving along, minding my business and not expecting any danger at all. The traffic light turned green, and I proceeded through the intersection. However, the oncoming car who was supposed to stop at her red light failed to do so. In fact, she didn't even slow down. I caught a glimpse of her car heading straight into me; an impact on the driver's side which surely would kill me. I saw that death was imminent, and I was ready to go on to be with the

Lord. I lifted my hands from the steering wheel, threw them straight up in the air, closed my eyes, and screamed, "*Jesus!*" to the top of my voice. I really thought it was all over. But it wasn't! Jesus took the wheel. When I opened my eyes, I was through the intersection and almost a half a block away. The one thing I know for sure is that I didn't touch the steering wheel, the gas pedal, or the brakes; I had surrendered. To this day, I don't know if I was actually transported or if Jesus guided the car with super speed into the right path to avoid the accident. I only know that I lived through that one.

The Breath of God

Once again, I faced death. I had a gall bladder attack and was rushed to the hospital and immediately sent into surgery. I didn't have time to think of anything before they had put me under the anesthesia. This was before they did gall bladder surgery with a laser, so I had to go under the knife. The surgery was successful, and they removed 176 small gallstones from me. The problem came after surgery; I was put on life support because I would not breathe on my own. All of my family had gathered at the hospital. It wasn't looking good for me. Every time they removed the equipment, I refused to breathe on my own. That was happening on the outside, but on the inside, I found myself underwater. The water was as clear as crystal, I could even see the little ripples moving in the water. There was a very brilliant light shining on the top of the water, and I knew if I could just get up to the top of the water and into the light, I could breathe. I wasn't gasping or struggling to breathe, and it didn't seem to bother me being underwater at all. I just had a very strong desire to get to the light at the top of the water. In my efforts to try to rise higher, I heard the voices of two nurses talking.

"Micki, you have to breathe, honey." Turning to speak to the other nurse, she said, "This just doesn't look good at all, she's still not breathing."

I guess they put the breathing tube back into me because everything was quiet for a while.

For just a brief moment, I saw the two women standing there with me. I also looked over to the machine registering my vitals. I just remember the number on my blood pressure was 30 over something, and then, I was gone again.

Once more, I heard the voices.

"You have got to try to breathe. Come on, Micki, and just try to breathe."

Everyone upstairs in my room kept praying for me. The next thing I remember is waking up in my hospital room. My friends, Flo and Rob, from out of state were standing at the foot of my bed. My family was there too, gathered around me, waiting anxiously for me to come back to them. It had been two days since my surgery.

God breathed life into Adam when he was created, and I believe God, in His love and mercy, breathed life into me again.

Glimpses of Eternity

As you have read my stories, you know that I have lived through many dangers. As I grew older, Satan attacked my body. I was a grandmother with two very beautiful granddaughters—Casi who was seven, and Brittany who was five. Oh, what a joy those girls were to me. Yes, I spoiled them as much as I could. We went on vacations together, planted flowers together, and enjoyed all of their birthdays and any other special days we could share. I loved them so much, and they really loved their grandma.

As I grew weak and my heart was giving me trouble, our times together slowed down a little, but we were still so very close. One Sunday morning, after church, I felt exhausted and thought it would be to my advantage to just lie down and rest a while. I remember crawling onto the bed still in my Sunday clothes and dropping my shoes to the floor as I fell face first into my pillows. But it didn't stop there; it seemed like I just kept falling right through the pillows and into another world. I was alive and very much awake as I found myself floating through the atmosphere. The cool moist clouds gently touched my cheeks. It was pleasant, it was quiet, and I was moving along slowly.

I found myself curiously looking around, when I noticed something bright and shimmering in the clouds to my right. I began to move closer for a better look. As I approached the beautiful lights like sparkling rainbows glittering in the distance, I became more and more anxious and excited. Soon, I could clearly see it was like a tunnel, but it was gently rotating around and around. Finally, I could really see what was happening. A beautiful tunnel had been formed in the sky. I gasped as I realized that the entire tunnel consisted of beautiful angels flying in perfect circles, as far as I could see, to form the tunnel. Beautifully and gently, they rotated, leaving the opening of the tunnel closer to me and the end of the tunnel in the distance, all angels—thousands of them. I was astonished. I stood still, looking into the tunnel. In the distance, I could see what appeared to be a white candle with melting wax, flowing from the candle with a bright golden flame burning. The candle was moving slowly through the beautiful angel tunnel toward me. As it came close to the end of the tunnel, I could see clearly. The brilliant white of the candle had transformed into the iridescent whiteness of the robes of Jesus Christ. The golden flame was now a wonderful, beautiful golden crown made up of thousands of smaller crowns entwined. I was looking into the warmest and softest eyes I had ever seen. It was wonderful and fearful at the same time. I heard myself speaking.

"It's the Lord!" I bowed my head in reverence.

My breath seemed to be taken away by the very awesomeness of His presence and appearance. When I could finally speak again, my voice was filled with reverence and anticipation as I lifted my head to speak to Him.

"Am I dying?"

There was silence as everything began to be revealed to me. I knew I wanted to go with the Lord; I wanted to go through that beautiful angel tunnel into paradise, but something, was tugging at my heart. I looked into the eyes of my Lord and said, "What about Casi and Brittany?"

Instantly, it was all over. I was back on my bed. This was no dream. My weakness had left me. I felt totally refreshed and renewed. (After all, I had been in the literal presence of my King.) I looked at my watch, and only ten minutes had passed. Ten minutes spent between Earth and eternity. My prayer is that when God desires to call me home on that final day, He will send Jesus and my angel tunnel.

* * * * *

There are more stories to be shared with you, but that will be for another time—hopefully in my next book. For now, it is my sincere desire that everyone reading these events will grow stronger in serving God in the capacities and places where He puts you. To be available and willing to be the hands, the voice, and the person that God uses you as one of the Creator's temporaries. You have been deployed by the King of kings, Lord Jesus, Himself, and your mission is possible. Payday's coming! Now, get to work. Are you ready for your assignment? Remember, you never have to do it alone! He is always there!

May God bless every person who reads this book and anoint them to answer His call.

Note: if you have had some of these instances in your life when you knew that only God controlled the situation, I would love for you to share those experiences with me. I am sure that God has many people on assignments, and maybe you are one of them.

mickicarpenter@ymail.com.

About the Author

Amelia Luzenne Barker, nicknamed Micki, was born in a small town in North Carolina, the daughter of Johnnie A. Barker and Sadie Harstin Barker. She is blessed with three sisters, Becky, Kathy, and Crystal; two sons, Hubert C. Jenkins, Jr. and Richard Scott Jenkins; husband, Charles E. Carpenter; and grandchildren and great-grandchildren.

When Micki was six years old, an old barracks building was put on some property just above their home. They all thought it would be a skating rink, but God had other plans. Rev. Lloyd T. Whidden established a church there. Micki and Becky attended regularly by themselves. They constantly begged their parents to go. Finally, one night, both parents attended a service and received the Lord Jesus into their hearts that night. The Barker family became a great part of that ministry. The following year, a new church building was built and dedicated as the *Oakwood Park Tabernacle, and later to become First Assembly of Gastonia, North Carolina*. Micki never missed a Sunday for thirteen years, straight. The church grew, and when Micki was eight years old, she played a major role as a little blind girl in the Christmas Drama and in many roles thereafter. At twelve, she became the church pianist, later as organist, a teacher, and youth leader. It inspired her for the life that was to follow.

Married at nineteen, within a few years, she became the mother of two sons. Her parents became ministers too. They established a church, *The Family Worship Center of Mount Holly, North Carolina,* where they ministered together for more than fifty years. Rev. Johnnie Barker also had a television ministry, *The Prophetic Message,* for fourteen years. Micki participated in everything that her parents did, teaching Sunday School, playing the piano, children's church, and she eventually pastored with her husband in South Carolina and North Carolina. During this time, she also helped with the production of her dad's television ministry. Micki wrote music, songs, and fourteen Christmas dramas which she produced and directed. Later, she and her husband, Charles Carpenter (known as Professor Diddledaddle), conducted The Carpenter's Kids Crusade through North Carolina and South Carolina. Her sisters participated in her dramatic plays and many crusades. This wonderful family was separated by the death of their mother on May 12, 2019, and, later, by the death of their father on June 14, 2019. All four girls continue to minister in God's services.

In addition to the fourteen Christmas dramas, Micki also worked for a publishing company, a newspaper, and authored a newspaper column called "And the Good News Is." She wrote the daily inspirational worldwide publication for the Union Gospel Press for one season.

Three children's books—*Casi's Country Christmas, Brittany's Best Gift, and The Adventures of David and Snowbell*—are soon to be published. When recalling the ways in which God has used her in her everyday life, Micki was inspired to write *The Creator's Temporary.* A book which will help you to realize that we are all on temporary assignment to do the work of our Savior in everyday places. We are appointed to work for His kingdom to come. You must be a child of God who is a willing witness to see His wondrous works unfold before your very eyes. We are His hands extended to others in this world who have needs that only you can meet by being open to the assignments given to you by the Heavenly Father, and it is only temporary.

9 781098 066277